W9-CGN-591

PERSONAL INCOME TAXATION

PERSONAL INCOME TAXATION

TAXATION

THE DEFINITION OF INCOME
AS A PROBLEM OF FISCAL POLICY

By HENRY C. SIMONS

THE UNIVERSITY OF CHICAGO PRESS

CHICAGO & LONDON

International Standard Book Number: 0-226-75892-3

THE UNIVERSITY OF CHICAGO PRESS, CHICAGO 60637

The University of Chicago Press, Ltd., London

PREFACE

THIS book perhaps combines strangely the characteristics of an academic treatise and a tract for the times. Attempting to serve both purposes, it may serve neither of them well. In any case, since several sections are addressed mainly to special students, some suggestions may be offered to other readers.

Much can be said for beginning with chapter x, which summarizes the argument and outlines a program for tax reform. Those who must read in haste may consult other chapters on a few topics of their own selection. No one should hesitate to skip parts of chapters i and iii which he finds tedious and unrewarding (pp. 6–15, 63–79, 90–96 esp.); and many readers, with a distaste for academic discussion, may simply omit these chapters.

I am somewhat apprehensive lest readers should find in this book an undue emphasis upon distributional considerations. Taxation is the proper means for mitigating inequality; and, confining attention to this field of economic policy, one naturally places more emphasis upon that objective than would be appropriate in a less restricted discussion. Besides, the reader may wisely make some allowance for the fact that several of these chapters were prepared originally with regard for prevailing opinions which, in both popular and academic circles, have since changed markedly. In spite of endless revising and re-writing, there are still some passages, notably in the introduction, which would have been more useful as contributions to discussion in the New Era than they will be now. When Republicans were the leading disseminators of economic fallacies, it was proper for the academic person to stress the problem of inequality. Nowadays, however, there is no issue as to the need for lesser concentration of wealth and income. Indeed, we tend now toward relative overemphasis, both in our talk and in our action, upon this particular objective.

On the other hand, there are now momentous issues as to the means by which inequality may properly or actually be mitigated—as to how we may diminish economic inequality without creating a greater inequality or monopoly of political power. A political discussion which has produced keen awareness of a problem has also rendered the community dangerously uncritical and undiscriminating as regards possible solutions. Almost any crank, mercantilist scheme can now be sold as a cure for excessive inequality; and the most naïve and preposterous "purchasing-power" arguments are employed by good people who, like our President, are ordinarily not unsophisticated. Fine sentiments about economic justice are now employed mainly in support of schemes which, in spite of all good intentions, must serve to aggravate inequality, to make poorer a community which at best will be poor enough, and to undermine a political system which we overwhelmingly prefer to the authoritarian alternatives. Thus, I would suggest, as the now significant interpretation of the argument in chapter i, not merely that progressive taxation is a sound and promising method for mitigating inequality but that it is the only sound and promising method which has seriously been proposed and that other currently popular schemes are unsound technically and incompatible with the kind of total arrangements which we wish to preserve against the recently prevailing world-trend.

Just as the Republican party consolidated its power by dispensing gigantic subsidies in the form of protective-tariff duties, so now the Democrats have been purchasing allegiance by endless restraints upon internal trade. Our politicians, having quietly and passively encouraged the proliferation of monopoly arrangements in many areas, now seek to promote and glorify these arrangements elsewhere. Thus, in the name of justice (fair wages, fair prices, parity prices, and other derivatives of the medieval conception), we are perverting and destroying the free enterprise, free markets, and competitive free trade which are essential to representative government and to orderly political life on a vast national scale. We are deliberately displacing competition within economic groups, which is essentially peaceful, orderly, productive, and mutually advantageous, by organized economic and political action which is inherently exploitative, destructive, and violent. Thus we move toward the politician's millennium where politics has crowded competition entirely out of the picture— toward the economy of organized negotiation which, once achieved, would immediately necessitate the induction of a supreme negotiator who, in turn, would either liquidate the organizations or utilize them to consolidate his own dictatorial powers. Along the same lines, of course, we are also moving directly away from the conditions which permit of peaceful and orderly relations among the nations of the world.

We need, at the present time, not greater awareness of inequality but greater awareness of the dangers involved in trying to mitigate it by methods which involve restraint of trade. Tax reform, with displacement of sales taxes, customs duties, excise taxes, and payroll levies by progressive personal taxes, would enable us to move gradually but steadily toward better distribution. Such reform can be accomplished within the framework of a democratic, competitive, free-enterprise system. It involves no threat of fundamental change in our institutions; and, instead of restriction of production, it promises increase in employment and in our total national income. In principle, much could be accomplished by more effective governmental spending, especially for education and other welfare services. In fact, however, it is hard to devise new spending schemes that will do more good than harm; and it is easy to impose or retain taxes which more than offset, by their regression and their augmenting of unemployment, any benefits which the expenditures may yield. In a world of large unemployment, it seems hard to mention any new governmental services which are worth the cost of the excise or payroll taxes that might be avoided or repealed if the services in question were withheld. Moreover, if it is hard to avoid bad forms of taxation, it is also hard to get enough taxes of any kind to protect against the inflation dangers of new spending schemes. Our economy can be rendered vastly more productive by the restoration of effective price competition; it can be rendered much more stable by movement toward a real monetary system; and, for the significant future, our attack upon inequality may properly be concentrated on changes in the taxes by which present expenditures are financed.

I regret that two recent books, which should be used and cited generously in a study of this kind, became available only after my manuscript was in its final form. The first of these is Roswell Magill's excellent legal study, *Taxable Income* (New York, 1936). This book covers admirably a phase of the subject which is only touched upon in my chapters, and one which, as the reader will discover for himself, I am both indisposed and incompetent to discuss systematically. The other book is a recent Twentieth Century Fund publication, *Facing the Tax Problem* (New York, 1937)—a very useful book which, by virtue of the contributions of Professors Haig and Shoup, is of first-rate importance for its discussion of income-tax problems. My opinions regarding the central points of that discussion have been summarized in a recent review (*Journal of Political Economy*, XLV [August, 1937], 532–35).

The following persons have each made large and generous contributions to the improvement of my manuscript at various stages: Professors Jacob Viner, Frank H. Knight, Simeon E. Leland, and Carl Shoup, and Mr. Aaron Director. I trust that this bare acknowledgment will not obscure my great indebtedness to these men; and I must apologize for not naming the many graduate students who have markedly influenced my thinking and helped to overcome my inhibitions about publication. (I cannot name them without risking errors of omission which would plague me afterward.) Professor Harry A. Millis has read the manuscript and made several excellent suggestions for change. Both he and Professor Gordon Laing have been helpful and encouraging as regards the arrangements of publication. Miss Gladys Hamilton contributed excellent stenographic services and discovered many errors which might otherwise have survived careful reading of the proof sheets.

For the protection of those who have helped me, be it said that each of them has suggested some changes which I was too indolent or too stubborn to make.

HENRY C. SIMONS

CHICAGO

TABLE OF CONTENTS

CHAPTER I

INTRODUCTION

ECONOMICS, as a separate discipline among the so-called social sciences, takes its rise and derives its essential meaning from specific problems of public policy. It deals, ultimately, with two kinds of practical questions: (1) What are likely to be the results of specified measures? (2) By what kinds of measures may specified results be attained? In its special branches, such as public finance, the main problems are obviously problems of "control"—problems of legislative policy, for the most part. Thus, the specialist in government finance becomes of necessity a sort of propagandist—a protagonist of "sound fiscal practices" and a hostile critic of measures which fall outside the pale. It is incumbent upon him, therefore, to set up fundamental objectives and criteria of fiscal policy. He must build upon a set of values—and these will usually be things which he brings with him to the special field, not end results of his specialized researches.

It has become conventional among students of fiscal policy, however, to dissemble any underlying social philosophy and to maintain a pretense of rigorous, objective analysis untinctured by mere ethical considerations. The emptiness of this pretense among economists is notorious; yet people who cannot solve a simultaneous equation still regard "unscientific" as the ultimate in critical invective and themselves live in constant terror of that characterization. Having been told that sentiments are contraband in the realm of science, they religiously eschew a few proscribed phrases, clutter up title-pages and introductory chapters with pious references to the science of public finance, and then write monumental discourses upon their own prejudices and preconceptions.

One means of avoiding this unfortunate procedure is to introduce at the outset a confession of faith or recital of preconceptions. For present purposes, brief discussion of the question of justice in taxation may adequately serve this end. We intend, in what follows, no real contribution to that subject,[1] or even a study of its extensive and exceedingly dull literature. It may be pos-

---

[1] A significant position regarding taxation and tax reform is properly a derivative, or subordinate part, of a broader position on general questions of economic policy. Taxation is only a small element in the structure of rules and conventions which constitute the framework of our existing economic system; and problems of taxation can be clearly apprehended only as phases of the broad problem of modifying this framework (the rules of the game) in such manner as to make the system more efficient and more secure. Those who reject revolutionary upheavals as a means to progress must analyze the shortcomings, the weaknesses, and the unlovely features of the system as it stands. They must determine which of its faults most urgently need correction and which are most easily amenable to correction. Finally, they must ascertain what kinds of measures are appropriate in each case. Thus, one's position regarding taxation can hardly be stronger than one's position on economic policy generally. Sound proposals for tax reform imply sound conception of the role of taxation changes in some larger scheme; they imply sound insights as to what tax reform may properly undertake to accomplish, and sound insights as to the urgent problems which may best be dealt with along other lines. At all events, the writer's argument regarding income taxation in these essays may properly be interpreted, and perhaps better understood, as part of a scheme of policy outlined in a short tract entitled *A Positive Program for Laissez Faire: Some Proposals for a Liberal Economic Policy* ("Public Policy Pamphlets," No. 15 [Chicago: University of Chicago Press, 1934]).

sible, however, to define some objectives of policy which will seem acceptable to many readers; at the least, subsequent chapters should be less unintelligible to one who understands the writer's tastes.

How tax burdens should be apportioned among individuals has no doubt been the subject of discussion and controversy since the beginning of political organization. So long as poverty and insecurity compel the sovereign to employ every available fiscal device in order to maintain sovereignty, questions of justice are naturally subordinate. Once stable government and a measure of economic freedom appear, however, considerations of equity are forced to the front. More revenue devices are available than are required. To what extent shall each kind of levy be employed? Questions of relative collection costs, of stability and flexibility of yield, are relevant of course. But, at the center, is the question of how the burden *should* be allocated, of what is the most equitable system.

A familiar answer to this question is found in the doctrine of taxation according to benefit. Each person may be called upon, as in his dealings with private enterprise, to pay according as he receives. It is fair to say, however, that this principle, with reference to the allocation of the whole tax burden, is now of interest only for the history of doctrine. It finds a diffident proponent here and there; but, on the whole, it has been repudiated as completely by students as by legislatures.

Taxation according to benefit, as a slogan, has an interesting history, which illustrates what a variety of uses and masters a good phrase may serve. In eighteenth-century France, when public expenditures were made largely with regard for the benefit of the tax-exempt nobility and clergy, it epitomizes a protest against obvious injustice. It was then a forward-looking doctrine, defining a proximate goal of liberal reform. Later on it serves those opposing the movement toward taxation of individuals differentially according to their circumstances; thus it becomes a significant element in a reactionary social philosophy, constructed from the gratuitous implications of laissez faire economics. And it still survives in the vigilant wisdom of the courts, protecting property against democracy.

The slogan, of course, has little more than emotive content. At best, it represents an ill-defined protest against obvious injustice (in the movement for "universality"); at worst, an empty evasive sort of conservatism (in the opposition to progression); but it defines no real basis for apportionment. In some cases, to be sure, its implications are fairly clear. Where the government distributes goods and services which may be bought and sold in the open market, pricing according to cost is feasible. Where expenditure is made for purposes of general welfare (national defense, internal security), the benefit principle leads nowhere at all; and, where the government undertakes deliberately to subsidize certain classes (the economically unfit) or certain kinds of consumption (education, recreation), taxation according to benefit is sheer contradiction.

On the other hand, one cannot deny the importance of benefit considerations for modern fiscal problems. Sound fiscal measures for the future must be designed, at many points, with regard (*a*) for the fact that particular classes will derive special benefits from certain kinds of government expenditure and (*b*) for what tax arrangements have been in the past. There is a decisive case for retention of a substantial element of *ad rem* taxation—for resort in part to levies which classify persons with respect to characteristics other than net income or net worth or "ability to pay."

The end of conciseness in argument will be served, if we leave the foregoing assertions for the present, without attempting to support them, and proceed to the problem of personal taxation. For purposes of this chapter, the general problem must be broken into three parts: (1) the problem of personal taxation; (2) the problem of *ad rem* taxation; and (3) the problem of the combination of these two types of levies in a complete system. To define the scope of discussion under (1), we may start by asserting that *ad rem* taxation should form an important, if minor, part of the system, and by assuming solution of the question as to what part of total revenues should be provided by levies in this latter form. Thus, we may proceed to the traditional question of justice in taxation.

The greater part of what has been written about justice in taxation has been couched in terms of sacrifice. This concept, along with "ability" and "faculty," is a more or less legitimate progeny of "utility"; and it has contributed about as much confusion, with respect to the ethics of public policy, as has "utility" with reference to the explanation of human behavior. Yet the doctrines built from and around these concepts deserve attention, if only because they are so firmly intrenched in the literature and even in lay discussion.

There is first the doctrine of equal sacrifice—that tax burdens should so be distributed that the same total sacrifice is imposed upon every individual. This we may associate with Mill, who asserts the position and then points out rather casually, as though it were axiomatic, that equal sacrifice among individuals means minimum sacrifice for the *community* as a whole.[2] This latter position has been subjected to devastating criticism at the hands of Mill's most sympathetic followers. Edgeworth, notably, turns the whole argument around, starting with the proposition that taxes should impose minimum total sacrifice; and he then demonstrates conclusively—so far as is possible with such dialectical tools—that equal individual sacrifice by no means minimizes the total burden.[3] Minimum sacrifice, as he demonstrates, calls for not equal but equimarginal sacrifice among individuals—i.e., for equality not in the total burden on each person but in the burden of the last small increment of tax. Intermediate between these positions, incidentally, is that of, notably, Cohen-Stuart, who contends that there should be equality of proportional sacrifice (proportional to the total utility of income!).[4]

Definite interpretation of these doctrines is exceedingly difficult. They all relate to taxation on the basis of income; and they surely involve the conception of a

---

[2] *Principles*, Book V, chap. ii, sec. 2.

[3] F. Y. Edgeworth, *Papers Relating to Political Economy* (London, 1925), Vol. II, chap. ii, pp. 100–125.

[4] See E. R. A. Seligman, *Progressive Taxation in Theory and Practice* (2d ed., 1908), pp. 278 ff.

functional relation between the amount of income and its marginal utility. Moreover, the area under the income-utility curve, or the integral of the function, is conceived to measure total utility. Sacrifice is defined as the loss of total utility.

Let us, then, postulate a generalized utility curve for "money income," i.e., a functional relation between amount of income and its marginal utility, applicable to all persons and to all income classes. If this curve be rather flat—if the arc elasticity be less than unity for all pairs of significant points—then equal sacrifice would mean regressive taxation, and proportional sacrifice would call perhaps for a mild sort of progression. If the curve were a rectangular hyperbola, proportional levies would produce equality of sacrifice.[5] All this, however, is not very illuminating. One derives practical implications from the criterion of equality, or proportionality, of sacrifice precisely in proportion to one's knowledge of something which no one ever has known, or ever will know, anything about. Perhaps this goes far toward explaining the popularity of these doctrines among academic writers.

It is a peculiar relative merit of the Edgeworth doctrine that it depends for some definite interpretation merely on the assumption that the utility curve has everywhere, within significant limits, a negative slope; and common sense, if it accompanies us at all in flight to such dialectical altitudes, will surely support this assumption. Thus, minimum sacrifice would appear to dictate a tax rate of 100 per cent, with an initial bracket

[5] See A. C. Pigou, *A Study in Public Finance* (London, 1928), p. 109.

of income exempt from tax, and with the level of exemptions adjusted according to revenue requirements.

This definiteness, however, is only apparent. To admit, as one must, the reality of differences in standards of living, is to concede that the simple income-utility function is only a locus of points on much steeper, "short-run" curves at the various income levels. The simple function tells us nothing about the proximate consequences for marginal utility to a normal Jones, if his income is changed from b to a. It only tells us what the marginal utility of the smaller (or larger) income will be to Jones *after* he has completely revised his standard of living, after he has become a thoroughly "a-dollar" man, and only after he has quite forgotten his better (or worse) days.   While these considerations do not dispose of the doctrine, or deny a certain relevance to the simple income-utility function, they do place the minimum-sacrifice legislator under the unfortunate disability of not knowing where to start.

Minimum-sacrifice doctrine, while proposing the outright slicing-off of income peaks, has yet the political wisdom to postpone that arrangement for an infinite period of time. It leads, under any reasonable assumptions as to the short-run functions, to progressive taxation; yet, while its sister-doctrines tell—quite equivocally—just how taxes should be apportioned, it says not only that taxes should be progressive now but also that they should be increasingly progressive for all time to come.

A system which produces least aggregate sacrifice this year will fail to achieve that result in the next fiscal year.

The marginal utilities of the large taxpayers will at first be indignantly high; but time will drag these utilities down toward the long-run utility curve as a limit. As taxpayers become adjusted to their new circumstances, their utility curves, like their indignations, will recede; and every such change will require an increase in the degree of progression. Thus, if the minimum-sacrifice principle were continuously applied, income differences would be in process of continuous moderation, with concomitant changes in standards of living and in the utility functions. Ultimately, it would give merely a confiscation of all income above a certain level—but only ultimately.

But there are further complicating considerations. The long-run income-utility function is itself a function of the prevailing distribution of income; and the short-run function for a member of any income class is one thing when other incomes remain unchanged and something quite different when all incomes within this and neighboring classes are changed concomitantly and systematically at the same time. The fact that consumption, especially in the upper-income classes, is so largely competitive and invidious constitutes by itself a powerful argument for steep progression. For the minimum-sacrifice program, it implies that the rates of tax should be much more progressive at the outset, and should be more rapidly increased afterward, than would otherwise be appropriate.

This consideration, as Pigou suggests, gives strong support to that persistent, but seemingly indefensible, notion that even equal sacrifice requires distinctly progressive levies. The loss of utility from curtailment of large incomes would be less great if that curtailment were general; or, in Pigou's words, "the satisfaction which a man derives from the possession of a given income depends, not only on the absolute amount of the income, but also on the relation subsisting between it and the incomes of other people."[6] At all events, the logic of least aggregate sacrifice leads far beyond the simple utility functions of Bernouilli and Cramer.

Minimum-sacrifice theory has done wonders toward sustaining the vitality of hedonism, at least in liberal economics. If we believe that science and logic point no highroad to justice and beauty, we still resent it; and, if we discourse on questions of policy, we dissimulate the conviction. We crave some ultimate sanction for our tastes and sentiments; at all events, we crave their company even within the "science" of finance. So, we invent and seize upon all manner of disguises—and even build up a professional code which frowns upon our not accepting some things merely for what they seem to be. Edgeworth and his followers have made good costumes; they have written our sentiments in a sort of logic; they have served a worthy cause and served it well. But from it all hedonism derives a blessing which is unearned and undeserved and, indeed, unfortunate for economics as a discipline.

What really commends the Edgeworth doctrine to liberal students, of course, is its conclusion—its pseudo-scientific statement of the case against inequality. Consequently, it is important to see that the doctrine de-

[6] *Ibid.*, p. 111.

rives not only all its practical implications but all its noble ethical quality from an assumption usually introduced or recognized without much ceremony. This is the assumption that all individuals are, or must be treated as, equally efficient as pleasure machines. Pigou disposes of the matter in two sentences:

> Of course, in so far as tastes and temperaments differ, allowance ought, in strictness to be made for this fact; . . . . But, since it is impossible in practice to take account of variations between different people's capacity for enjoyment, this consideration must be ignored, and the assumption made, for want of a better that temperamentally all taxpayers are alike.[7]

To a person who found Professor Pigou's conclusions uncongenial, this method of reaching them simply by confession of ignorance might seem absurdly easy. Such a person might maintain, not unfairly, that this confession, far from reconciling hedonism and equalitarianism, really implies that they belong to different universes of discourse.

The conclusions, to be sure, may be salvaged to some extent by proper amendment of the premises. Instead of merely professing ignorance, one might maintain (a) that there is no presumption favoring the existence of significant positive correlation between individuals' incomes and their respective efficiencies as pleasure machines; (b) that such differences as exist merely because the income distribution has been what it has been may be ignored for long-run policy; (c) that the assumption of equality in original, innate capacities for pleasure is a sufficiently precise approximation to the facts; or (d)

[7] *Ibid.*, p. 76.

that no other assumption is either politically practicable or morally tolerable. The last argument would evidence frankness and candor; but it invites suspicion of logical legerdemain. Certainly it would reduce the whole hedonistic calculus to a merely superfluous embellishment of the argument. The other premises, to many persons, will therefore seem more inviting. For votaries of hedonistic welfare economics, however, they all have the disadvantage of revealing the crucial importance of this step in the argument.

Indeed, one may well insist that hedonistic ethics is not less absurd than hedonistic "explanation" of human behavior, or less naïve than the productivity ethics which we associate with J. B. Clark. This latter brand of apology, though somewhat out of fashion now, deserves a moment's attention, even at risk of laboring the obvious.

Let us imagine a competitive economy, without inheritance, where all persons have substantially equal talents for straight thinking, imagination, salesmanship, and chicanery, but are enormously unequal in physical strength. Here, of course, the millionaires will be the persons with strong backs; and the apology of productivity ethics will be that they are entitled to share in the social income according to their respective differential contributions (productivity). A dose of Calvinist theology would make this doctrine more palatable to the masses; but persons of a critical temper might be led to restate the implications and to revise the conclusions simply by reversing them. If a person has been greatly favored by the Creator in the dispensation of rare physical blessings, it is hard to regard that initial good fortune as a basis for preferential claims against his fellows with respect to scarce goods whose distribution is amenable to some deliberate, human control. Indeed, one is almost obliged to admit the reasonableness of the opposite system of ethical bookkeeping, whereby rare physical blessings would be debited to the recipient's account with the universe. Let us now build up the analogy with respect to hedonistic welfare economics.

Let us imagine a world where people, while substantially equal in other respects, display enormously different efficiencies as pleasure machines. Let us imagine also that these efficiencies vary inversely as the cube of the cephalic index. In such a world the criterion of least aggregate sacrifice would require that taxation leave the longheads with very large incomes; and a consistent policy would require that all impecunious longheads be generously subsidized. Now, to support such a scheme, one finds an appropriate theology not only convenient but utterly indispensable. The criterion implies that the primary objective of policy on earth should be that of generating *through* the human population the maximum output of pleasure for the contemplation of some external Spectator; and the appropriate supporting religion would assert that this Spectator dispensed blessings and punishments to humanity according to the adequacy of the pleasure output.

A critical, disinterested Spectator, contemplating such a world, would probably conclude, however, that the ethical claims of the longheads were, if anything, weaker and more specious than those of the strongbacks in the other world. If a person obtains, by virtue of luck or divine favoritism in the dispensing of genes, a remarkably efficient mechanism for converting income into pleasure, would not a meticulously equitable system equalize as between him and his fellows not marginal or incremental utility but simply total utility? It might seem somewhat ungenerous and vindictive for his fellows to insist upon such an arrangement; and the corollary implications respecting the treatment of the roundheads would sorely try economists' souls. But a deity could hardly be called unjust if he built a world on this general pattern. At all events, if the longheads succeed in getting and keeping as large incomes as the roundheads, they would do well to rest content. Certainly they should try to discourage speculative inquiries into questions of justice.

If there is any cogency in these remarks, one may conclude that the case for equality (for less inequality) is enormously stronger than any utility foundation on which it can be rested; indeed, that hedonistic ethics, no less than productivity ethics, shrivels almost to absurdity when confronted with the creed of "the greatest good *of the greatest number.*" To grant this is to demand that hedonism, repudiated as a basis of explanation of human behavior, be denied domicile in the "economics of welfare."

Such a demand will fall, in many quarters, upon deaf ears. Many professors of economic dialectic still find comfort and intellectual satisfaction (and "filler" for courses and textbooks) in the "explanations" of hedonism; and a larger group will continue to practice a kind of utility therapy and to write their prescriptions for the economist's millennium in the hedonistic code. But serious students of fiscal policy and fiscal therapy cannot afford to achieve callousness to that always disturbing, and usually fruitful, question: What of it? Unless they can find some intelligible reasons for trying to maximize total social utility or to minimize aggregate sacrifice, they will do well not to spend their lives trying to define the conditions under which these ambiguous ends would be realized.

More sensible and more important than the contributions of utility theorists is the so-called sociopolitical theory of Adolph Wagner. Wagner contends, in effect, that taxation must be conceived as an instrumentality for altering or correcting the distribution of wealth and income and, what is more important, that only in this light do maxims of taxation according to ability or faculty or sacrifice have any real meaning. He would say that, if one regards the prevailing distribution of wealth and income as the only righteous, just, or expedient distribution, then it is idle to talk about ability to pay, to defend progression, or even to support the exemption of small incomes. His views (if we pursue them no farther) seem eminently sensible and represent sound criticism of other writers.[8]

Wagner's candor and clarity on these points have exposed his position to many adverse comments; and some writers have found his doctrine a too severe test of their tolerance. Seligman, to take an extreme case, deals with

[8] See Wagner, *Lehrbuch der politischen Oekonomie*, VI, Theil II (2d ed., 1890), 381–85 *et passim*.

Wagner most severely and, in so doing, has considerably influenced American opinion. The cogency of Seligman's criticism, and his facility with emotive language, may fairly be judged from two statements which seem especially revealing:

It [Wagner's doctrine] would land us not only in socialism, but practically in communism.[9]

Legal justice means legal equality, and a legal equality which would attempt to force an equality of fortune in the face of inevitable inequalities of native ability would be a travesty of justice.[10]

The first statement requires no comment; and the second, if one looks behind the obvious ambiguity, reveals an unquestioning acceptance of the productivity ethics which we have referred to above.

The passages are quoted from Seligman's *Progressive Taxation in Theory and Practice.* Here the author, after roundly condemning the notion that improvement of the income distribution is a proper objective of tax policy, goes on to argue, in the very next paragraph, that public expenditures may properly be directed to attainment of that end. This conviction that expenditure is a proper instrumentality for controlling the income distribution but that taxation must not so be conceived is surely an amazing achievement of academic reflection. Nor is it less amazing that Seligman should argue strongly, later

[9] *Op. cit.,* p. 131. Seligman was taken to task severely by H. C. Adams for his discussion of Wagner. See Adams, *Science of Finance* (New York, 1898), p. 342 n.

[10] Seligman, *op. cit.,* p. 132. Actually this quotation follows the first edition (Publications of the American Economic Association, Vol. IX, Nos. 1 and 2, p. 69). In the second edition, the phrase "equality of fortune" becomes "inequality of fortune"; but the change is undoubtedly a typographical error.

on, for progression, on the grounds that it is required by his totally ambiguous "principle" of taxation according to faculty.[11]

Such curious methods of defending progression are commonplace. The practice typically is that of admitting progression through the back door, under the cloak of Adam Smith's first maxim. Tons of paper have been employed in teaching the world that taxes should be levied according to ability—perhaps for the reason that this word utterly defies definition in terms of any base upon which taxes are or ever might be levied. Whereas the question is as to how taxes should be allocated with respect to income, consumption, or net worth, the answer is that they should be proportional to ability or faculty, which cannot be conceived quantitatively or defined in terms of any procedure of measurement. Such an answer indicates that the writer prefers the kind of taxation which he prefers; that he is unwilling to reveal his tastes or examine them critically; and that he finds useful in his profession a basic "principle" from which, as from a conjurer's hat, anything may be drawn at will.

To avoid dissimulation and circumlocution, one may begin by saying what one thinks about inequality. Indeed, one may assert a substantially equalitarian position; or, at least, that there is a presumption in favor of equality and that the burden of proof rests with him who would depart from it. With such a start, one may hold that every increase in the degree of progression is, *with reference merely to distributional effects*, a desirable

[11] *Ibid.*, Part II, chap. iv.

change, and without limit short of substantial equality among those taxed. The same position may be acceptable even to persons not sympathetic toward a thoroughgoing equalitarianism, for the existing distribution may bear no trace of the *kind* of inequality which they approve. And all the practical implications may commend themselves to cautious critics committed only to the view that inequality is sadly excessive here and now.

At any rate, it may be best to start by denying any justification for prevailing inequality in terms of personal desert. This position has the great virtue of being definite; and it seems more nearly defensible than any other simple position relevant to the immediate problem. If one refuses to accept this dogma, one's error cannot be demonstrated by resort to scientific or dialectical analysis. We may plead, remonstrate, preach, and exhort; but we cannot prove. But one dogmatic assertion is permissible, namely, that by no other means can the problem be dragged out into the open. Taxation must affect the distribution of income, whether we will it so or not; and it is only sensible to face the question as to what kinds of effects are desirable. To do this is to reduce the discussion frankly to the level of ethics or aesthetics. Such procedure, however, is certainly preferable to the traditional one of "describing" the attributes of the good life in terms which simply are not descriptive.

The case for drastic progression in taxation must be rested on the case against inequality—on the ethical or aesthetic judgment that the prevailing distribution of wealth and income reveals a degree (and/or kind) of inequality which is distinctly evil or unlovely.

Such a view obviously takes account merely of the distributional effects of progression. Indeed, that is as far as traditional discussions of justice in taxation may properly go. Yet this is obviously but one side of the problem. The degree of progression in a tax system may also affect production and the size of the national income available for distribution. In fact, it is reasonable to expect that every gain, through taxation, in better distribution will be accompanied by some loss in production. The real problem of policy, thus, is that of weighing the one set of effects against the other.

Two simple points should be noted at the outset. First, the effect of a higher degree of progression in taxation upon the distribution of income is certain; the effect upon production, problematical. One is a matter of arithmetic; the other, largely, of social psychology. Second, if reduction in the degree of inequality is a good, then the optimum degree of progression must involve a distinctly adverse effect upon the size of the national income. Prevailing opinion to the contrary notwithstanding, it is only an inadequate degree of progression which has no effect upon production and economic progress.

But what are these sources of loss, these costs of improved distribution? There are possible effects (a) upon the supplies of highly productive, or at least handsomely rewarded, personal services, (b) upon the use of available physical resources, (c) upon the efficiency of enterpriser activity, and (d) upon the accumulation and growth of resources through saving. Of these effects, all but the last may be regarded as negligible, under any degree of progression which is at all likely to obtain; at least, this position is not indefensible, and surely it is a lesser distortion of the truth than the essentially opposite position so commonly implicit in popular discussion and in the writings of conservative economists.

The attractiveness of jobs as jobs surely varies, on the whole, directly and markedly with the remunerations which they carry. What competing firms must pay to get experts away from one another is vastly different from what society would be obliged to pay in order to keep the experts from being ditch-diggers. Physical resources it will always be more profitable to employ than to leave idle, so long as progression falls short of 100 per cent or does not rise precipitously to that level. Our captains of industry (enterprisers) are mainly engaged not in making a living but in playing a great game; and it *need* make little difference whether the evidence of having played well be diamonds and sables on one's wife or a prominent place in the list of contributors under the income tax. Besides—and this may be emphasized—the mere privilege of exercising power is no mean prize for the successful enterpriser.[12]

[12] This is not the place for more cautious and judicious discussion of the economic effects of income taxes. What would otherwise be careless and offensive dogmatism is perhaps justified where the main purpose is that of revealing the writer's biases and, in particular, of presenting the tentative conclusion that, within significant limits, only the possible effects on capital accumulation are of first-rate importance. More thorough treatment would consider especially the possible effects upon investment in more venturesome undertakings, i.e., on the gambling aspects of enterprise. It seems, however,

These remarks define, of course, an extreme and not wholly tenable position. But the adverse effects of increasing progression may be estimated only in terms of predictions of human behavior; and one may well doubt that most of them would be important, at least under any degree of progression which is politically possible or administratively practicable for the significant future. With respect to capital accumulation, however, the consequences are certain to be significantly adverse. How increased progression would affect the *incentive* to accumulation or saving, it would be rash to predict. Here the ultimate question is essentially that of the probable effect of small changes in the rate of interest upon the rate of saving. That the incentive, within wide limits of tax practice, would be unaffected, is as reasonable as any

----

that too much importance is likely to be attached to such effects. In the first place, some deterrent against the more uncertain and risky commitments might well be economically salutary. In spite of our obvious indebtedness to those who have been wisely venturesome in the past, one feels that modern social and economic arrangements are conducive to an excessive wagering of resources at long odds, to overrapid development of new areas, and to undue haste in the exploitation of new technical discoveries which, with only a little more delay and patience, might be adopted and applied (or discarded) with great reduction of the relevant uncertainties. The mere existence of commercial gambling is significant evidence on this score; and a careful accounting of our total outlays in prospecting for gold and oil would probably be very illuminating. Second, if the effect of progressive, personal taxes on speculative investments is undesirable, it is attributable in no small measure to gross defects of existing taxes which are easily amenable to correction. Our tax laws are crude, niggardly, and patently unfair in their treatment of losses. With these defects removed (see chaps. vii and x below), the possibility of deducting losses would largely counterbalance the prospective tax on speculative gains, except for persons and enterprises whose small resources prohibit diversification of investments. At the worst, some measure of inhibition against long-odds ventures is a perhaps inevitable, but relatively unimportant, cost of more equitable tax arrangements.

other position, many economists to the contrary not-withstanding.[13]

Nevertheless, it is hardly questionable that increasing progression is inimical to saving and accumulation. Under an individualistic system, great inequality is necessary to rapidly increasing indirectness in the productive process—necessary to the increasing use of resources in the production of more (and different) resources. The cost of our present stock of productive instruments was, in a significant sense, decades and centuries of terrible poverty for the masses. Conversely, the cost of justice will be a slowing-up in our material advance (though this effect may be modified if and as governments assume the role of savers).

Increasing progression means augmenting incomes where saving is impossible and diminishing incomes too large to be used entirely for consumption. Thus, it means diversion of resources from capital-creation to consumption uses. The classes subject to the highest rates will not greatly curtail consumption; and persons at the bottom of the income scale, paying smaller taxes, will use their additional income largely to improve their standard of life. Some curtailment of consumption at

[13] As Schmoller argued so clearly, the rate of saving would appear to depend on many other factors more intimately than upon the rate of interest. Certainly it will depend upon the prospects with reference to the security of the institution of property and of the whole economic and political system. Moreover, mitigation of the grosser inequalities in the distribution of income, wealth, and power would surely fortify the existing system against attack and contribute to the prospects of its stability and security. Thus, highly progressive taxation might serve, historically, to sustain and strengthen the incentive to accumulation. See G. Schmoller, "Die Lehre vom Einkommen in ihrem Zusammenhang mit den Grundprinzipien der Steuerlehre," *Zeitschrift für die gesamte Staatswissenchaft*, Vol. XIX (1863), *passim*.

the upper end of the scale may be expected, as may some increase of saving at the lower end. That the net effect will be increased consumption, however, hardly admits of doubt.

Here perhaps is a real cost, a limitation, a poser for one who would lead us away from extreme inequality via taxation. Increased saving is a true blessing, other things being equal;[14] its curtailment, undeniably a loss. Nevertheless, the position that progression should be applied only moderately, because of its effect upon ac-

[14] Of course, saving may be a real affliction during a depression. When unfavorable cost-price relations discourage investment, an increase of saving will aggravate hoarding and thereby aggravate maladjustments between the flexible and sticky prices. In such periods, incidentally, the income tax has great advantages over other taxes, by virtue of its effect on saving, and because it does not contribute to the cost-price maladjustments. No other important type of levy can be imposed with less adverse effects per dollar of revenue.

Many devotees of "oversaving" theories would argue, of course, that the adverse effects of progression upon saving are desirable or even necessary for purposes of fuller or more stable employment. We repudiate this argument entirely; and we wish scrupulously to avoid the temptation, which must face every ardent advocate of progression, to support his case by recourse to sophistries of the kind recently propagated by Mr. Keynes in England and, more journalistically, by David Cushman Coyle in this country. One may concede that their arguments contain an obscure element of practical insight and are more nearly respectable intellectually than earlier doctrines of oversaving. Our economy is more dangerously exposed to catastrophic deflation than to excesses in the opposite direction; and, historically, we have had perhaps less increase in the quantity and/or velocity of money than would have been ideal. Urgent as is the need for a sound program of monetary reconstruction, however, it seems improper to regard progressive taxation as a part of such a program. To concede that increase in money turnover is often, if not typically, desirable is not to argue for every kind of measure which would operate in this direction. Those who advocate progressive taxes, because they curtail hoarding by curtailing saving, seem to take no account (1) of the need for minimizing monetary uncertainty through the establishment of definite rules of policy, (2) of the need for rigid economy in the kinds of devices for implementing those rules, or (3) of the need for sharp focusing of respon-

cumulation, is by no means inviting when one considers precisely what it means.

There is, first of all, a question as to whether society should make large sacrifices to further accumulation. To stress obligations to our children's children is often a means of diverting attention from patent obligations to our contemporaries. For the future there is a responsibility of maintaining a respectable proportion between population and resources—which surely admits of more than one method. Of course progress should be encouraged; but its costs should give us pause, in a society mature enough to exercise some deliberate control. Both progress and justice are costly luxuries—costly, above all, in terms of each other. Let us raise the question, in passing, as to whether we have been quite safely removed from the predicament of that hypothetical soci-

---

sibility for observance of the rules. Moreover, such taxes, as a device for controlling the velocity of money, have the disadvantage of working only in one direction; at any rate, no one appears to advocate their reduction or abolition in boom times as a means for checking a movement of dishoarding!

The advocates of these intriguing heresies appear to argue that we cannot afford prosperity because additional income promotes hoarding; but the paradox, however salable and entertaining, is intellectual rubbish. One means for reducing hoarding, to be sure, is to keep people very poor. The excuse for killing of the goose, however, is very lame. There is no need for restricting saving in order to restrict hoarding; appropriate monetary rules, implemented by mandatory changes in the quantity of money, can assure adequate (or excessive) spending by making the alternative cost of hoarding as high as may be necessary, and without any deliberate diversion of funds from would-be savers to the more profligate or necessitous. Thus, to paraphrase a previous statement, the case for progression is enormously stronger than any monetary considerations on which it might be rested; and those who seek to support it in this way only raise doubts about an otherwise strong position.

For statement of the writer's views on monetary questions see "Rules versus Authorities in Monetary Policy," *Journal of Political Economy*, XLIV, No. 1 (1936), 1–30. See also chap. x, Addendum, below.

ety which employed every increase in its income for the purposes of further increase, and so on until the end of time.

There is also a difficult question, from the point of view of the economics of welfare, as to the relative importance of productional and distributional considerations. There is real point, if not truth, in the suggestion that, within wide limits, the quality of human experience would be about the same at one income level as at another if the *relative* position of persons and classes remained unchanged. Poverty, want, and privation are in large measure merely relative. Thus, something can be said for mitigation of inequality, even at the cost of reduction in the modal real income.

It is important to recognize that each generation inherits a system of property rights, as well as a stock of means of production—that it receives its resources with mortgages attached. If we deliberately limit the degree of progression, out of regard for effects on accumulation, we are in effect removing taxes from those who consume too much and transferring them to classes which admittedly consume too little; and against the additional capital resources thus painfully acquired are mortgages, property rights, in the hands of those freed from tax. While the saving will really have been done by those at the bottom of the income scale, those free from tax and their assigns will enjoy the reward. This method of fostering increase in productive capacity thus increases the concentration of property and aggravates inequality.

If the productivity of capital were highly elastic—if the long-period demand for investment funds were not extremely elastic—the phenomenon of diminishing returns might be relied upon to mitigate the distributional effects. The masses would surely participate to some extent in the blessings of greater productive capacity. In fact, however, the scheme looks a bit like taxing small incomes to reduce consumption in the hope that those relieved of tax will save more after consuming all they can, and then allowing 1 per cent to those who have really done the saving and 4 per cent to those who have served merely by paying smaller taxes. We are thus placed under the strange necessity of lamenting the flatness of the productivity curve—of lamenting the otherwise glorious prospect of using additional capital goods very productively. The anomaly arises, of course, merely from the institution of property, which largely sets the distributional problem of taxation.

A possible solution of this difficulty is budgetary provision for capital accumulation on the part of governments. In this way, fiscal policy might promote or sustain accumulation without incurring the doubly unfavorable terms involved in restricting progression to that end. Whether and how far this is really feasible are questions of political morality and administrative efficiency. The same questions arise when one asks how large government expenditures should be and, indeed, are at the heart of the problem of social control through fiscal devices. If governments can administer and effectively direct the production and distribution of certain classes of goods and services, expenditures and taxation may properly be high. If governments could handle effectively the business of investment, more drastic measures for modifying the degree of inequality would be desirable and expedient.

Opportunities for extending the scope of socialized consumption are clearly numerous. Many goods and services, of great importance for general welfare, might be distributed freely or with substantial relaxing of prevailing price controls. The prospect for public administration of saving is much less promising. For the immediate future, however, the retirement of public debts will provide an adequate offset to the adverse effects of progression on saving;[15] and, after debts were entirely retired, governments might still contribute somewhat to the volume of savings available for private investment by adhering to a pay-as-you-go policy. Moreover, they might proceed gradually with investment in private industry.[16] The techniques of a conservative investment business are fairly well established; and govern-

[15] No case can be made for lowering the higher surtaxes, in order to foster saving, when this proposal contemplates reduction in the rate at which the government debt is being retired, for the taxation and expenditure together will in this case increase rather than diminish the amount of funds available for private investment. At least it is highly probable (almost certain) that a larger proportion of the funds will be saved if transferred to bondholders in exchange for their bonds than if left in the hands of the taxpayers.

[16] Here, again, there are some immediately attractive opportunities, especially in the case of the public utilities. Regulation is a peculiarly unsatisfactory and anomalous expedient, justifiable only on the dubious grounds that governments are more nearly competent to regulate than to own and operate. Under a sound, long-term program, the government, while undertaking to preserve competitive controls for industry as a whole, should plan gradually to acquire and operate those industries where competition simply cannot serve as an implement of control. At least, there would seem to be no proper place for regulation of private industry (as to prices and investment) under anything like our existing economic system or under anything like democratic government.

mental bodies might, on a moderate scale, function quite as well as the investment departments of the better banks and insurance companies. Considerable investment might be made without involving the government in the management of private business—just as governments may distribute all sorts of consumption services while leaving many steps in their production in the hands of private enterprise. Indeed, governments might well remain, special cases apart, in a quite passive, creditor role, merely dispensing investment funds according to interest return and security.

To the inevitable protest that this means socialism, one may reply that the program is properly part of a promising scheme for saving the free-enterprise system and the institution of political freedom.[17] The growth of government investment in private industry might be thoroughly gradual; steps could be taken forward or backward according to the dictates of expediency; and

[17] These paragraphs were written years ago, at a time when the writer was less sensitive to the difficulty or impossibility of maintaining representative government in the face of increasing centralization and collectivism. Complete revision has not seemed necessary, however, for, although the shades of emphasis are sometimes unfortunate, the central position seems sound. The direct provision by governments of capital funds for private industry is something which can be viewed only with grave misgivings. However, if we were faced with a dangerous tendency toward capital consumption and disaccumulation, such a policy would seem preferable to that of making taxes less progressive (or more regressive) than otherwise would have been expedient. Actually, it is altogether academic to consider how the government might find adequate outlets for its own saving, with our present debt, and with great industries which can never be effectively competitive still under private ownership. To suggest that the government might protect our capital resources by assuming the role of saver is not to suggest that it become even a passive investor in competitive, private industries during the next century!

perhaps the maintenance of accumulation would not justify or require continued saving through the government. The contention here is not that there should be correction of the effects of extreme progression upon saving but that government saving, rather than modification of the progression, is the appropriate method for effecting that correction, if such correction is to be made.

Any such scheme implies increasing reliance upon political controls. The vital issues in economic policy, however, have to do with the form of political control rather than with its extent, for increase is inescapable. Moreover, the control of the distribution of income through taxation represents a form of control which democratic governments can be expected to exercise somewhat correctly, i.e., without undermining the foundation of their own existence. No fundamental disturbance of the whole system is involved. Business would still be conducted for profit; the prosperous would still exercise power; the game should remain substantially as interesting and attractive as ever; and the control of relative prices might still be left to the forces of competition.

Under this kind of program, governments might gradually abandon the passive, creditor role and, as it seemed expedient, undertake the actual administration of industries; but, the case of the "natural monopolies" apart, it need never be so. It would be possible to go as far in this direction as seemed advisable at any particular time; and the cumulative effect of policies over long periods might be a substantial change in the economic system. The program, however, is infinitely elastic. Every step might be tested on its merits. Thus fiscal devices may be regarded as the most promising means to desirable change in the economic system—and for the reason that they permit of that gradualness which seems indispensable to sound achievements.

The problem of justice in personal taxation has another important aspect. It is never possible, in practice, to define, establish, or adhere closely to an ideal tax base. We must recognize possibilities of discrimination —even though the task of defining it is rather baffling. Neglecting the good *ad rem* levies, we may say that tax burdens should bear similarly upon persons whom we regard as in substantially similar circumstances, and differently where circumstances differ. This may seem like waste of words; but the point is important. It furnishes much of the case against such programs as the single tax; and important criticisms of existing tax instruments are in the nature of protests against this indefinable something which we call "discrimination." What such criticisms mean will appear more clearly as we examine special problems of income taxation. At all events, if we are to tax different economic classes in a widely different manner, we must devise equitable techniques for defining classes and for locating taxpayers in the proper classes. Fiscal devices employed with broad objectives of control must be sharp instruments.

Even these general remarks require qualification, however. An ideal income tax should involve a minimum of obvious inequity; and the writer believes that, in general, the broadest and most objective income concept provides the base for the most nearly equitable levies. At many points, however, one is tempted to repudiate an objective criterion or to disregard its dictates. Such concessions are often the part of wisdom and sound policy. But there is always danger in a practice of compromising, say, between the requirement that taxation shall mitigate an objective sort of inequality and the requirement that relative levies on individuals shall find approval in some sense of reasonableness. For this latter test leads directly back into the utter darkness of "ability" and "faculty" or, as it were, into a rambling, uncharted course pointed only by fickle sentiments. Sentiments of fairness cannot be ignored; but, on occasion, one does well to maintain that income taxes should diminish the inequality of income, letting the chips fall where they may.[18]

The preceding discussion has to do with one aspect of the problem of tax apportionment, namely, the financing of expenditures properly chargeable against the whole community. Such expenditures should be financed, we submit, with regard primarily for the distributional effects of the levies.[19] There remains now the question as to the proper scope of nonpersonal or *ad rem* levies—as to how large a part of total government expenditures may properly be covered by levies which in-

[18] See below, esp. chap. vi.

[19] The writer does not contend that the personal income tax is the only levy which should be used to cover such expenditures. Certainly a case may be made for supplementing the income tax with a progressive, personal tax based on total wealth or individual net worth. Inheritance taxes, however, should probably be consolidated with the income tax. On this latter point see below, chaps. vi and x.

volve no direct regard for distributional considerations (i.e., for the total income circumstances or total wealth of the taxpayer). This question will be dealt with briefly, since it is not closely relevant to our present task.

Whether particular activities should be financed out of general revenues is obviously an unsatisfactory test of whether they should be undertaken by governmental bodies. It is thoroughly appropriate, in principle, that the state should perform services for particular groups in the community where there is no occasion or justification for subsidizing them. Moreover, many things done primarily for the general welfare will also involve special advantage to particular classes from which compensation may equitably and expediently be exacted.

This means, of course, that proper distribution of the burdens of government expenditure cannot adequately be considered apart from the actual uses of government funds. One must know what the state does in order to discuss intelligently how revenues should be obtained. Moreover, one must know how taxes have been levied in the past.

The substantial case for *ad rem* levies rests on two grounds: (1) The imposition of such levies in the past has, in some cases, established vested interests which it would be inequitable to disturb now by reduction of these levies and (2) the current activities of governments confer special benefits upon particular classes, where the classes are not regarded as proper objects of subsidy, and where special levies upon them are feasible.

There is a substantial element of truth in the maxim that "old taxes are good taxes." In a free-enterprise system it is important that there should be considerable stability in the "rules of the game," and taxes are an important part of those rules. All nonpersonal taxes affect the direction of private investment, and all changes in such taxes will create "windfalls" of gain or loss. In the case of excises and tariff duties, however, these considerations do not argue strongly against change but only in favor of allowing a period for readjustment before the changes become effective. With reference to taxes on real property, on the other hand, they argue perhaps against any change at all—or even in favor of such increase of effective rates as might reasonably have been anticipated.

The case is clearest, of course, with respect to urban sites. Here the state has, in effect, established a substantial equity. Sites have been bought and sold at prices which have contemplated continuance of taxes at roughly the prevailing rates—just as they have been bought and sold subject to mortgage claims. The very arguments which seem decisive against the program of the single tax are, indeed, also decisive against concessions by the state with respect to that equity which it has definitely established by taxation in the past.[20]

[20] This is not to say that no case can now (1934) be made for reduction of taxes on real estate. In depression periods the average percentage of assessed value to true value undoubtedly rises somewhat in most communities; and, where this occurs, a convincing case can be made for reduction of the nominal rate of tax. But no good case can be made for reduction in the true, effective rate. The plight of real estate owners gives a sort of plausibility and political strength to movements for drastic lowering or limitation of the rates of tax; and it should be understood that such measures involve a most unjustifiable change in the rules of the investment game.

Real estate taxes may be regarded merely as obligations under a special kind of mortgage held by the state. Reduction of the rates of tax below pre-

With respect to other forms of real property (buildings, agricultural land), the case is practically the same, although slightly different in principle. The effective rates of tax might be changed without serious inequities if a long period were allowed for readjustment before the change became effective. But it is hardly worth considering the possibilities of allowing widely different "readjustment periods" for different kinds of property (different as to "durability" or rate of reinvestment); and tax legislation would be politically ridiculous if its effective date were placed decades after the date of enactment. Thus, in a nation where real-property taxes have become firmly established, these levies should probably be retained permanently at the established level.

The case for retention of benefit levies in the tax system rests partly on considerations of equity, partly on considerations of political expediency, and partly on considerations of economy. The equity considerations may be suggested by referring to an extreme case. Suppose that the state controls the production and distribution of some commodity (say, tobacco) which is widely consumed, but consumed in very different quantities by different individuals and not consumed at all by a large fraction of the community. Now it would obviously be

---

depression levels would be defensible only as part of a scheme for scaling-down all debts, regardless of the circumstances of the debtors. Present holders of real estate assumed an obligation to pay taxes, just as some assumed mortgages. If it be argued that their investments have turned out badly, the same may be said of other investments where people merely poured in their own funds (savings). All this can hardly be undone now, without causing more inequity than is corrected; and, if a case can be made for relief of debtors generally, highly differential and special concessions to people as debtors to the state remain thoroughly objectionable.

inequitable and improper here for the state to sell the commodity below cost; and, conceding this, one concedes the case with respect to benefit levies in general. Their justification is to be found simply in the presumption against special subsidies—whether to people as consumers of a particular commodity or to people as owners of real estate which rises in value by virtue of public improvements.

The political considerations are equally obvious. Suppose that a new arterial highway is to be constructed into a developing suburban area. If no benefit levels are in prospect, the competent legislature is left with the task of choosing the particular group of property owners who shall prosper by virtue of the decision as to location. It is thus likely that the actual choice of location will be determined (a) by the opportunities for consolidating the position of a dominant political machine in marginal areas or (b) by the size of bribes or campaign contributions offered by different groups of real estate owners. At all events, the financing of such a project in part by levies on the property peculiarly benefited would surely be conducive to healthier political life.

The economic considerations will be suggested by the same instance, for the imposition of benefit levies would be conducive to more nearly "correct" location. Let us consider here the case for such levies in connection with the construction of a municipal electric railway to serve a suburban area. In this instance it is important to note that people will actually pay for the service in question, partly as they actually use it (in fares) and partly in the form of higher rents in areas accessible to the service.

Now the establishment of the service in question will become economically feasible (will return interest at the prevailing rate), in the absence of benefit levies, only when interest and operating costs are covered by the prospective fare revenue; but it will become economically advantageous (sound) as soon as the total payments for actual service *and for access to service* suffice to cover interest and operating expense.[21] In many instances, moreover, the appropriate benefit levies would permit of service at lower fares.

All this has to do, obviously, with special assessments and special taxes (uniform property taxes over "benefit areas"). If it is clear that such levies have great merit from several points of view, it is almost equally clear that they present enormous difficulties in application, for there are and can be no very satisfactory techniques either for determining total "benefit" to property or for allocating the charges over particular parcels in accordance with relative benefit.

In the case of many special assessments the difficulties have been minimized by virtue of establishment of standard practices in different communities. With re-

[21] Critical readers may argue that, in such cases, the possible adverse effects upon rental values in competing areas should be taken into account. Some kinds of worsements doubtless should be recognized in the calculation; but one must be careful not to adopt here, by implication, the criteria of resources allocation which would be dictated under monopoly. To deduct all pecuniary worsements, direct and indirect, is to repudiate the equal-productivity criterion and to accept, as guides of economic policy, marginal revenue in lieu of price and marginal expense of the industry in lieu of marginal expense of the plant or firm. Many of the indirect worsements seem closely analogous to the effects of production by a new firm, in a competitive industry, upon the product price obtained by other firms and upon the prices of their various items of input.

spect to kinds of improvements (or services) which are rather uniformly distributed over wide areas, it matters little what the bases for allocating charges happen to be, provided they have become traditional and have been understood by persons acquiring and disposing of real estate. Here, again, one can fall back on the comfortable position that old taxes (arrangements) are good merely by virtue of their being old.

With respect to such things as new parks, boulevards, and school buildings, however, the otherwise decisive case for benefit levies is seriously weakened by the fact that benefit simply cannot be measured—that no useful principles can be laid down with reference to the task of measurement. Application of the benefit principle implies estimates of what property values would have been in the absence of the improvement and of what they will be after the improvement is made. Thus, it is one thing to say that levies should be allocated in accordance with benefit; and it is something else (apparently impossible) to specify in principle how this result may be achieved. If benefit taxation is seen merely as differential taxation of real estate according to the particular judgments or interests of particular legislatures, it loses much of its appeal. In the case of larger and less common improvements even the most competent and scrupulously honest estimates as to property benefit involve guesses and extrapolations which will almost certainly prove grossly wrong.

The strong arguments in favor of such levies, however, would appear to justify their continued employment, in spite of these difficulties. Perhaps the best that could be hoped for is that considerable stability in methods of allocating assessments might gradually be attained with respect to the commoner types of improvements.

It remains to mention another special instance in which benefit considerations support the *ad rem* type of levy—the case of the gasoline tax. (Taxonomically, this may be regarded as a special case in the pricing of particular public services, comparable to the tobacco case already noted.) Governments, constructing enormous networks of hard-surfaced highways, are thereby providing special services to persons as owners of pleasure cars and to enterprises employing motor transport (and to their customers). Since there can be no justification of deliberate subsidy either to the use of pleasure cars, or to persons as owners of pleasure cars, or to one form of commercial transportation as against others, there is the strongest case on both political and economic grounds for the imposition of special charges. The obvious system of toll charges, however, has been abandoned for good reasons; and the gasoline tax has been hit upon as an excellent device for accomplishing indirectly, and with a minimum of administrative difficulty and personal inconvenience, what it is inexpedient to attempt directly. The case is interesting as a rare instance in which a decisive argument can be made for a commodity tax.

While it seems clear that good fiscal arrangements will allow an important place to *ad rem* levies, it is obviously impossible to make significant generalizations as to the percentage of total revenues which they should

provide. However, it should be noted that the considerations which have been advanced in support of such
taxes are applicable to only a few of the many *ad rem*
levies which are and have been imposed; few of the existing nonpersonal taxes have any justification at all, except that they provide revenue.

It may be useful to submit, in concluding, a hasty
characterization of existing tax systems in the light of
the argument of this chapter.

There is in the United States one good form of personal tax, the progressive tax on personal income, which
ordinarily contributes less than 10 per cent of all revenues. There are good *ad rem* taxes in the form of the
tax on real property, special assessments and special
taxes, and gasoline taxes, not to mention the numerous
sources of nontax revenue which might be regarded as
ad rem charges. Except for the estate and inheritance
taxes (which should be consolidated with the income
taxes), this about exhausts the list of taxes which can
be defended in terms of broad considerations of fiscal
policy. The remaining "miscellaneous category" contains taxes of all degrees of "badness." Some, like the
tax on corporate incomes, simply lack justification in
terms of the positive considerations emphasized here,
neither contributing to inequality nor involving gross
diseconomies. At the other extreme are the tariff duties
and the various excises on commodities, especially the
tobacco and liquor taxes[22]—all of which distort the eco-

[22] Many liberal persons defend levies like the tobacco tax on the curious
grounds that tobacco is not a necessity—that poor people may or can avoid
the burden by not consuming the commodity. This position invites two comments. First, it is hardly accurate to say that no burden is involved in getting

nomic allocation of resources and contribute enormously to the degree of inequality. Somewhere in between
may be located the numerous miscellaneous excises and
license fees.

Probably no convincing case can be made for substantial extension of the place of the good *ad rem* levies
in the whole system. Those which are justifiable merely
because well established cannot justifiably be decreased
or increased; and the reliance on strictly benefit levies
must obviously be rather limited. Thus, the cleaning-
up of the great miscellaneous category of bad and worse
taxes depends upon extension of the strictly personal
levies. The transition to a fiscal system in which every
tax would have some substantial justification would appear, therefore, to require increasing the contribution of
the personal income tax many fold; indeed, to a point
where it would cover considerably more than half of
total governmental expenditures. A personal income
tax yielding, say, eight billions annually would represent
a most difficult achievement; but it is by no means
utopian.

---

along without the commodity. Second, it seems a little absurd to go around
arguing that poor people could or ought to do without tobacco, especially if
it is taxed, in the face of the facts that they simply do not do anything of the
kind, that the commodity was selected for taxation because they are not expected to do so, and that the government would not get much revenue if they
did. The plain fact, to one not confused by moralistic distinctions between
necessities and luxuries, is simply that taxes like the tobacco taxes are the
most effective means available for draining government revenues out from
the very bottom of the income scale. The usual textbook discussions on these
points hardly deserve less lampooning than their implied definition of luxuries
(and semiluxuries!) as commodities which poor people ought to do without
and won't.

CHAPTER II

THE DEFINITION OF INCOME

THE development of income taxes may be viewed as a response to increasingly insistent and articulate demand for a more equitable apportionment of tax burdens.[1] These taxes are the outstanding contribution of popular government and liberal political philosophy to modern fiscal practice. Thus, they may properly be studied in the light of considerations raised in the preceding chapter. Income taxation is broadly an instrument of economic control, a means of mitigating economic inequality. In what follows, we shall assume that moderation of inequality is an important objective of policy and proceed to consider income taxes as devices for effecting it. We shall be concerned, that is to say, largely with problems centering around that elusive something which we call "discrimination." Income taxes, in general, may seem peculiarly equitable; but serious problems arise when one proceeds to the task of describing, delimiting, and defining closely the actual tax base. Here, too, the problems may be dealt with largely in the light of considerations of justice.

We must face now the task of defining "income." Many writers have undertaken to formulate definitions,

[1] For stimulating development of this thesis see W. Moll, *Über Steuern* (Berlin, 1911), pp. 3–46. See also Bruno Moll, *Probleme der Finanzwissenschaft* (Leipzig, 1924), *passim*. The latter writer remarks (p. 99): "Vermögens- und Einkommensbegriff entspringen der gleichen Wurzel, dem Begriff des wirtschaftlichen Könnens, dem Vermögensbegriff im weitesten Sinne."

and with the most curious results. Whereas the word is widely used in discussions of justice in taxation and without evident confusion, the greatest variety and dissimilarity appear, as to both content and phraseology, in the actual definitions proposed by particular writers. The consistent recourse to definition in terms which are themselves undefinable (or undefined or equally ambiguous) testifies eloquently to the underlying confusion.

The fact that the term is widely used without serious misunderstanding in certain ranges of discourse, however, is significant. Since it is widely agreed that income is a good tax base, its meaning may be sought by inquiring what definition would provide the basis for most nearly equitable levies. At the same time we may seek to point out conflicts and contradictions in established usage and to discover the connotations of income which are essential and relevant for present purposes. Thus we may find those denotations which may best be accepted, to avoid ambiguity, and to minimize disturbance of terminological tradition.

What is requisite to satisfactory definition of income will appear clearly only as we come to grips with various problems. It may help, however, to indicate some general requirements—if only because their neglect has been responsible for so much careless writing in the past. Income must be conceived as something quantitative and objective. It must be measurable; indeed, definition must indicate or clearly imply an actual procedure of measuring.[2] Moreover, the arbitrary distinctions im-

[2] The importance of this requirement may be suggested by the following definition: "Net individual income is the flow of commodities and services

plicit in one's definition must be reduced to a minimum. That it should be possible to delimit the concept precisely in every direction is hardly to be expected.[3] The task rather is that of making the best of available materials; for no very useful conception in "social science," or in "welfare economics," will entirely satisfy the tough-minded; nor can available materials so be put together as to provide an ideal tax base. But one devises tools of analysis which are useful, if crude; and a tax base may be defined in such manner as to minimize obvious inequities and ambiguities. Such at least is the present task.

The noun "income" denotes, broadly, that which comes in. Thus, it may be used with almost any referent.[4] Even in the current usage of economics and business the term is commonly used in different contexts to denote several different things. It will suffice here to

---

accruing to an individual through a period of time and available for disposition after deducting the necessary costs of acquisition" (W. W. Hewett, *The Definition of Income* [Philadelphia, 1925], pp. 22–23). The author never undertakes to specify how this conception might be reduced to quantitative expression; he simply leaves the reader to guess how "the necessary costs of acquisition" might be deducted from "the flow of commodities and services accruing," or how either of these "quantities" might be arrived at separately.

[3] Kleinwächter, notably, endeavors to discredit the whole concept of income by pointing out that some arbitrary delimitations are unavoidable (*Das Einkommen und seine Verteilung* [Leipzig, 1896], pp. 1–16). He confounds himself and his reader with interesting conundrums having to do mainly with income in kind. See below, esp. chap. v.

[4] For discussion of the development of the income concept see Kleinwächter, *op. cit.*, Introduction; also, Bruno Moll, *op. cit.*, esp. chap. xii; also Bücher, *Zwei mittelalterische Steuerordnungen* (Fests. z. Leipziger Hist. [1894]), pp. 138–39 (cited in B. Moll, *op. cit.*, p. 96).

note three or four distinct senses in which the term is employed.

There is, first, and most common in economic theory, the conception of what may be called *income from things*.[5] In this sense, income may be conceived in terms of services derived from things or, quantitatively, in terms of the market value of uses. Thus, we speak commonly of income from land, from produced instruments, or from consumers' capital. When used in this way, the term may have a merely acquisitive implication; for any property right, any mortgage against the community, has its yield.

The term is also frequently used to denote, second, *gain from transactions* or trading profit. If a share of stock is purchased for $100 and later sold for $150, it is customary to say that the venture has yielded an income of $50. The distinguishing feature of this conception is that it presupposes no allocation of income to assigned periods of time—that it does not raise the often crucial question as to when "income" accrues.[6] The period is merely the time between the first and last transactions in a complete and mutually related series. "Income" is imputed neither to preassigned time intervals nor to persons but merely to certain ventures, certain market operations.

There is, third, the familiar conception of *social or*

[5] This is nicely covered by the German *Ertrag*—which most writers distinguish (some, carefully and consistently) from *Einkommen*. The *Ertrag* conception is that commonly employed (e.g., by Irving Fisher) in analysis of the discounting process (see below, chap. iii, pp. 89 ff.).

[6] Actually, it is always misleading to talk about the accrual of income. See below, pp. 99–100.

national income—which appears frequently in the literature and is often defined after a fashion.[7] Social income denotes, broadly, a measure of the net results of economic activity in a community during a specified period of time. This, of course, is no definition; indeed, it is perhaps impossible to do more than indicate some roughly synonymous, and equally ambiguous, expressions. While commonly employed as though it denoted something quantitative, social income cannot be defined to any advantage in strictly quantitative terms. Economics deals with economy; economy implies valuation; and valuation is peculiarly and essentially relative. The prices with which rigorous economics deals are pure relations; and relatives cannot be summated into meaningful totals. Market prices afford only the most meager clues (or none at all) to the "value" of *all* goods produced and services rendered.

The concept of production, moreover, has itself a strong ethical or welfare flavor. The social income might be conceived in terms either of the value of goods and services produced or of the value of the productive services utilized during the period (after deduction for depreciation and depletion).[8] On neither basis, however,

[7] "The aggregate money income of a country . . . . must equal the aggregate money value of all goods produced and services rendered during the year" (R. T. Ely, *Outlines of Economics* [4th ed.; New York, 1923], pp. 100 and 105). One may remark upon the failure to introduce depreciation or depletion into the calculation. The necessity of such deduction is recognized in Alfred Marshall, *Principles of Economics* (8th ed.), p. 81; but Marshall's conception of social income is nowhere made explicit.

[8] This view is developed especially in Cassel, *The Theory of Social Economy*, trans. Barron (New York, 1932), chaps. i and ii. See also the same author's *Fundamental Thoughts on Economics* (New York, 1925).

is it possible to avoid the question as to whether all economic (acquisitive) activity may be deemed productive. The use of resources to establish monopoly control can hardly be thought of as adding to the income of the community as a whole; nor is it easy to include the cost of the more egregious frauds perpetrated upon consumers. The tough-minded economist may argue that advertising is merely a service demanded by consumers— that an advertised product is simply a different commodity from a physically identical article with no distinctive label on the container; and this may solve the difficulty for one interested in the mechanics of the pricing process. But even a person of such interests will hesitate to maintain that all selling devices, truthful, false, and ludicrous, contribute to the social income. Large amounts of resources are employed to conceal issues in elections and to secure favor with actual and prospective government officials. But the point need not be labored. Surely it is impossible to distinguish sharply between uses of resources which involve production, predation, and mere waste. Such distinctions, however, are implicit in the idea of social income.

In short, social income is merely a welfare conception. To say that it has increased is to say that things which must be economized are more abundant (or, perhaps, are utilized with greater "efficiency"). This manifests an ethical or aesthetic judgment. Increase in the social income suggests progress toward "the good life," toward a world better in its economic aspect, whatever that may be; and it is precisely as definite and measurable as is such progress.

If it be true that social income belongs far outside the realm of rigorous, quantitative concepts, the conclusion is important for the definition of *personal income*—a fourth sense in which the term is commonly used. Many writers imply or assert explicitly that personal income is merely a derivative, subordinate concept in the hierarchy of economic terminology. The view that personal income is merely a share in the total income of society is to be found in almost every treatise on economics; and some writers, forgetting even the distinction between a real and a personal tax (and that between *base* and *source*), insist that income taxes must bear—presumably by definition!—only on the net social income as it accrues to individuals.[9] On this view, gifts, capital gains, and other items must be excluded from the base of a personal tax because such items cannot be counted in the income of society as a whole!

Such notions derive, perhaps, from the central emphasis placed upon national income by Adam Smith and the mercantilists and from the central place of so-called distribution theory in classical economics. Economists have discussed the influence of trade policy upon the size of the national income; they have broken up that income curiously into functional elements; indeed, they have done almost everything with the income concept except to give it such definition as would make it eligible to a place among our analytical tools. As a matter of fact, traditional theory is concerned primarily not with *Einkommen* but with *Ertrag*—with the pricing of goods

[9] E.g., Walther Lotz, *Finanzwissenschaft* (1st ed.; Tübingen, 1917), pp. 444–50.

and productive services. Its acquaintance with *Einkommen* is tenuous, implicit, and largely incidental.[10] Social income is neither an indispensable analytical tool for relative-price theory nor a concept whose content must be specified implicitly by a sound system of theory. At all events, no writer, to our knowledge, has succeeded in giving any real meaning to the idea that personal income is merely a share in some undistributed whole. The essential point has been most happily phrased by Schmoller, who says in an early work, "Nach unserer Ansicht gehört der Einkommenbegriff aber überhaupt streng genommen nur der Einzelwirtschaft an, der Volkswirtschaft nur in bildlich analoger Ausdehnung."[11] Certainly much should be gained by cutting loose from a terminology ambiguous at best and inherited from the discussion of problems largely, even totally, irrelevant to those with which we are here concerned.[12]

[10] For discussion of this point see A. Ammon, "Die Begriffe 'Volkseinkommen' und 'Volksvermögen' und ihre Bedeutung für die Volkswirtschaftslehre," *Schr. d. Verein für Sozialpolitik*, CLXXIII, 19–26.

[11] G. Schmoller, "Die Lehre vom Einkommen . . . . ," *Zeitschrift für die gesamte Staatswissenschaft*, XIX (1863), 78. Schmoller himself actually defines national income as the sum of all individual incomes (*ibid.*, p. 20) but in such context that one may hardly charge inconsistency.

[12] Most of the innumerable German discussions of the meaning of income start with, and pretend to lean upon, Hermann, who was concerned primarily with the concept of social income, and who certainly did not write from the point of view of taxation (as do his "followers"). See Hermann, *Staatswissenschaftliche Untersuchungen* (2d [posthumous] ed.; München, 1870), esp. chap. ix.

In Germany the "correction" of Adam Smith's overemphasis upon the "accounting" conception of social income ("ausschliesslich in dem von Standpunkte des capitalistischen Unternehmers berechneten Ueberschusse das reine Einkommen zu erblicken," is Robert Meyer's characterization of

Although personal income is not amenable to precise definition, it has, by comparison with the concept of social income, a much smaller degree of ambiguity. Its measurement implies estimating merely the *relative* results of individual economic activity during a period of time. Moreover, there arises no question of distinction between production and predation. Social income implies valuation of a total product of goods and services; while personal income is a purely acquisitive concept having to do with the possession and exercise of rights.

Personal income connotes, broadly, the exercise of control over the use of society's scarce resources. It has to do not with sensations, services, or goods but rather with rights which command prices (or to which prices may be imputed). Its calculation implies estimate (*a*) of the amount by which the value of a person's store of property rights would have increased, as between the beginning and end of the period, if he had consumed (destroyed) nothing, or (*b*) of the value of rights which he might have exercised in consumption without altering the value of his store of rights. In other words, it implies estimate of consumption and accumulation. Consumption as a quantity denotes the value of rights ex-

Smith's "narrow" conception [*Das Wesen des Einkommens* (Berlin, 1887), p. 3]) is regarded as a major contribution of German economics. Schmoller and most writers after him give credit to Hermann for this contribution. Meyer (*ibid.*, chap. i) insists, however, that Schmoller has found in Hermann the opposite emphasis from what is really there and that credit for the contribution belongs really to Schmoller (and to Rodbertus). The controversy is hardly important for present purposes in any event, for the present writer's position implies, so far as concerns the definition of personal income, that Schmoller to some extent, and his followers especially, erred simply in getting away from Smith.

ercised in a certain way (in destruction of economic goods); accumulation denotes the change in ownership of valuable rights as between the beginning and end of a period.

The relation of the income concept to the specified time interval is fundamental—and neglect of this crucial relation has been responsible for much confusion in the relevant literature. The measurement of income implies allocation of consumption and accumulation to specified periods. In a sense, it implies the possibility of measuring the results of individual participation in economic relations *for an assigned interval* and without regard for anything which happened before the beginning of that (before the end of the previous) interval or for what may happen in subsequent periods. All data for the measurement would be found, ideally, within the period analyzed.

Personal income may be defined as the algebraic sum of (1) the market value of rights exercised in consumption and (2) the change in the value of the store of property rights between the beginning and end of the period in question. In other words, it is merely the result obtained by adding consumption during the period to "wealth" at the end of the period and then subtracting "wealth" at the beginning. The *sine qua non* of income is *gain*, as our courts have recognized in their more lucid moments—and gain *to* someone during a specified time interval. Moreover, this gain may be measured and defined most easily by positing a dual objective or purpose, consumption and accumulation, each of which may be estimated in a common unit by appeal to market prices.

This position, if tenable, must suggest the folly of describing income as a flow and, more emphatically, of regarding it as a quantity of goods, services, receipts, fruits, etc. As Schäffle has said so pointedly, "Das Einkommen hat nur buchhalterische Existenz."[13] It is indeed merely an arithmetic answer and exists only as the end result of appropriate calculations. To conceive of income in terms of things is to invite all the confusion of the elementary student in accounting who insists upon identifying "surplus" and "cash."[14] If one views society as a kind of giant partnership, one may conceive of a person's income as the sum of his withdrawals (consumption) and the change in the value of his equity or interest in the enterprise. The essential connotation of income, to repeat, is *gain*—gain *to* someone during a specified period and measured according to objective market standards. Let us now note some of the more obvious limitations and ambiguities of this conception of income.[15]

In the first place, it raises the unanswerable question as to where or how a line may be drawn between what is and what is not economic activity. If a man raises vege-

[13] Quoted by Schmoller (*op. cit.*, p. 54) from Schäffle, "Mensch und Gut in der Volkswirtschaft," *Deutsche Vierteljahrschrift* (1861).

[14] This point, with all its triteness, can hardly be overemphasized, for it implies a decisive criticism of most of the extant definitions of income. Professor Hewett, e.g., asserts and implies consistently that income is merely a collection of goods and services which may, so to speak, be thrown off into a separate pile and then measured in terms of money. He and others too, no doubt, know better; but, when one undertakes the task of definition, one may expect to be held accountable for what one literally says. For other instances of this fallacy see below, chap. iii.

[15] Most of the points raised in the following pages will be dealt with again in succeeding chapters as problems of income taxation.

tables in his garden, it seems clearly appropriate to include the value of the product in measuring his income. If he raises flowers and shrubs, the case is less clear. If he shaves himself, it is difficult to argue that the value of the shaves must also be accounted for. Most economists recognize housewives' services as an important item of income. So they are, perhaps; but what becomes of this view as one proceeds to extreme cases? Do families have larger incomes because parents give competent instruction to children instead of paying for institutional training? Does a doctor or an apothecary have relatively large income in years when his family requires and receives an extraordinary amount of his own professional services? Kleinwächter suggests[16] that the poorest families might be shown to have substantial incomes if one went far in accounting for instruction, nursing, cooking, maid service, and other things which the upper classes obtain by purchase.

A little reflection along these lines suggests that leisure is itself a major item of consumption; that income per hour of leisure, beyond a certain minimum, might well be imputed to persons according to what they might earn per hour if otherwise engaged. Of course, it is one thing to note that such procedure is appropriate in principle and quite another to propose that it be applied. Such considerations do suggest, however, that the neglect of "earned income in kind" may be substantially offset, for comparative purposes (for measurement of relative incomes), if leisure income is also neglected. For

[16] *Op. cit.*, Introduction. We have drawn heavily, in this and other passages, on Kleinwächter's conundrums.

income taxation it is important that these elements of income vary with considerable regularity, from one income class to the next, along the income scale.

A similar difficulty arises with reference to receipts in the form of compensation in kind. Let us consider here another of Kleinwächter's conundrums. We are asked to measure the relative incomes of an ordinary officer serving with his troops and a *Flügeladjutant* to the sovereign. Both receive the same nominal pay; but the latter receives quarters in the palace, food at the royal table, servants, and horses for sport. He accompanies the prince to theater and opera, and, in general, lives royally at no expense to himself and is able to save generously from his salary. But suppose, as one possible complication, that the *Flügeladjutant* detests opera and hunting.

The problem is clearly hopeless. To neglect all compensation in kind is obviously inappropriate. On the other hand, to include the perquisites as a major addition to the salary implies that all income should be measured with regard for the relative pleasurableness of different activities—which would be the negation of measurement. There is hardly more reason for imputing additional income to the *Flügeladjutant* on account of his luxurious wardrobe than for bringing into account the prestige and social distinction of a (German) university professor. Fortunately, however, such difficulties in satisfactory measurement of relative incomes do not bulk large in modern times; and, again, these elements of unmeasurable psychic income may be presumed to vary in a somewhat continuous manner along the income scale.

If difficulties arise in determining what positive items

shall be included in calculations of income (in measuring consumption), they are hardly less serious than those involved in determining and defining appropriate deductions. At the outset there appears the necessity of distinguishing between consumption and expense; and here one finds inescapable the unwelcome criterion of intention. A thoroughly precise and objective distinction is inconceivable. Given items will represent business expense in one instance and merely consumption in another, and often the motives will be quite mixed. A commercial artist buys paints and brushes to use in making his living. Another person may buy the same articles as playthings for his children, or to cultivate a hobby of his own. Even the professional artist may use some of his materials for things he intends or hopes to sell, and some on work done purely for his own pleasure. In another instance, moreover, the same items may represent investment in training for earning activity later on.

The latter instance suggests that there is something quite arbitrary even about the distinction between consumption and accumulation. On the face of it, this is not important for the definition of income; but it must be remembered that accumulation or investment provides a basis for expense deductions in the future, while consumption does not. The distinction in question can be made somewhat definite if one adopts the drastic expedient of treating all outlays for augmenting personal earning capacity as consumption. This expedient has little more than empty, formal, legalistic justification. On the other hand, one does well to accept, here as elsewhere, a loss of relevance or adequacy as the necessary cost of an essential definiteness. It would require some temerity to propose recognition of depreciation or depletion in the measurement of personal-service incomes —if only because the determination of the base, upon which to apply depreciation rates, presents a simply fantastic problem. It is better simply to recognize the limitations of measurable personal income for purposes of certain comparisons (e.g., by granting special credits to personal-service incomes under income taxes).

Our definition of income may also be criticized on the ground that it ignores the patent instability of the monetary *numéraire;*[17] and it may also be maintained that there is no rigorous, objective method either of measuring or of allowing for this instability. No serious difficulty is involved here for the measurement of consumption—which presumably must be measured in terms of prices at the time goods and services are actually acquired or consumed.[18] In periods of changing price levels, comparisons of incomes would be partially vitiated as between persons who distributed consumption outlays differently over the year. Such difficulties are negligible, however, as against those involved in the measurement of accumulation. This element of annual income would be grossly misrepresented if the price level changed markedly during the year. These limitations of

[17] See Jacob Viner, "Taxation and Changes in Price Levels," *Journal of Political Economy*, XXXI (1923), esp. 494–504.

[18] In a sense relevant to income measurement, two persons' consumption of, say, strawberries might be very unequal for a period, though the physical quantities involved were identical, provided one consumed them largely in season and the other largely out of season.

the income concept are real and inescapable; but it must suffice here merely to point them out. (Their significance for income taxation will be considered later on.)

Another difficulty with the income concept has to do with the whole problem of valuation. The precise, objective measurement of income implies the existence of perfect markets from which one, after ascertaining quantities, may obtain the prices necessary for routine valuation of all possible inventories of commodities, services, and property rights. In actuality there are few approximately perfect markets and few collections of goods or properties which can be valued accurately by recourse to market prices. Thus, every calculation of income depends upon "constructive valuation," i.e., upon highly conjectural estimates made, at best, by persons of wide information and sound judgment; and the results of such calculations have objective validity only in so far as the meager objective market data provide limits beyond which errors of estimate are palpable. One touches here upon familiar problems of accounting and, with reference to actual estimates of income, especially upon problems centering around the "realization criterion."

Our definition of income perhaps does violence to traditional usage in specifying impliedly a calculation which would include gratuitous receipts. To exclude gifts, inheritances, and bequests, however, would be to introduce additional arbitrary distinctions;[19] it would

[19] The greater part of the enormous German literature on *Einkommenbegriff* may be regarded as the product of effort to manipulate verbal symbols into some arrangement which would capture the essential connotations of *Einkommen* (as something distinct from *Ertrag*, *Einnahme*, *Einkünfte*, etc.),

be necessary to distinguish among an individual's receipts according to the intentions of second parties. Gratuities denote transfers not in the form of exchange —receipts not in the form of "consideration" for something "paid" by the recipient. Here, again, no objective test would be available; and, if the distinctions may be avoided, the income concept will thus be left more precise and more definite.[20]

It has been argued that the inclusion of gratuities introduces an objectionable sort of double-counting. The practice of giving seems a perhaps too simple means for increasing average personal income in the community. But philosophers have long discoursed upon the blessings of social consciousness and upon the possibilities of improving society by transforming narrow, acquisitive desires into desire for the welfare of our fellows. If it is not more pleasant to give than to receive, one may still hesitate to assert that giving is not a form of consumption for the giver. The proposition that everyone

provide a not too arbitrarily delimited conception, and yet decisively exclude gifts and bequests. It is as though an army of scholars had joined together in the search for a definition which, perfected and established in usage, would provide a sort of "linguistic-constitutional" prohibition of an (to them) objectionable tax practice. For summary of this literature see Bauckner, *Der privatwirtschaftliche Einkommenbegriff* (München, 1921). See also below, chap. iii.

Of course, we must avoid the implication that our definition establishes any decisive presumption regarding policy in income taxation. The case for or against taxation of gratuitous receipts as income ought not to be hidden in a definition. See below, chap. vi.

[20] The force of the foregoing argument is perhaps diminished when one remembers that the distinction creeps in unavoidably on the other side of the transaction—i.e., in the distinction between consumption and expense in the case of the donor. But there remains a presumption against introducing the distinction twice over if once will do.

tries to allocate his consumption expenditure among different goods in such manner as to equalize the utility of dollars-worths may not be highly illuminating; but there is no apparent reason for treating gifts as an exception. And certainly it is difficult to see why gifts should not be regarded as income to the recipient.

The very notion of double-counting implies, indeed, the familiar, and disastrous, misconception that personal income is merely a share in some undistributed, separately measurable whole.[21] Certainly it is a curious presumption that a good method for measuring the relative incomes of individuals must yield quantities which, summated, will in turn afford a satisfactory measure of that ambiguous something which we call social income. This double-counting criticism, in the case of some writers (notably Irving Fisher), carries with it the implied contention that all possible referents of the word "income," in different usages, must be definable or expressible in terms of one another. We have pointed out several different usages of the term in order to show that they represent distinct, and relatively unrelated, conceptions—conceptions which only poverty of language and vocabulary justifies calling by the same name.

[21] Some writers explicitly avoid the implication that social income should be definable in terms of individual incomes or vice versa: Held, *Die Einkommensteuer* (Bonn, 1872), chap. iv, esp. pp. 92 ff.; F. J. Neumann, *Grundlagen der Volkswirtschaft* (Tübingen, 1899), pp. 220–21; Schmoller, *op. cit.*, p. 78; Ammon, *op. cit.*, pp. 21–26; Meyer, *op. cit.*, chap. xii.

CHAPTER III*

OTHER DEFINITIONS AND THEIR LIMITATIONS

THERE are few treatises on general economics which do not present some sort of definition of income. These definitions usually appear in the early pages, as part of introductions which seldom introduce, and rarely find any place in the more rigorous chapters which follow. Indeed, they are really not definitions at all but merely somewhat synonymous phrases which leave the underlying conception at least as ambiguous and unprecise as it would have been in the beginner's mind if he had proceeded immediately with the chapters on value and price. Most economists seem to define income, and no end of other terms, in their introductions just to have it over with and never put their concepts to the crucial test of use in careful argument. Few of them define personal income with regard to any special use of the concept, for theory or for practice; fewer still, with regard for problems of taxation.

Such, at all events, is our apology for narrowing considerably the range of inquiry in the present chapter. The problem which concerns us has come in for little

* Most readers probably should omit this chapter or reserve it for later examination. One may proceed directly from chap. ii to chap. iv without sensing much discontinuity. Those who lack facility with German may not find the following pages altogether unrewarding; but only the first half of chap. iii involves frequent quotations from German writers; and the latter half (pp. 79 ff.) may be read independently.

discussion in English and American economics; and what literature one finds is in small measure the product of minds distinguished for their acumen. Indeed, one may focus attention merely upon some half-dozen writers. In Germany, however, a long and spirited controversy begins at least as early as Schmoller's remarkable article in 1863[1] and persists unabated at the present time. The controversy has mainly to do with the implications of theory for tax policy; and almost every German prominent in *Nationalökonomie* and *Finanzwissenschaft* has taken an active part. So, it will be necessary to range wider in the German literature, if only to indicate the position of leading proponents of different doctrines.

At least two writers have sponsored conceptions of income which coincide substantially with that presented in the chapter preceding. Georg Schanz, the distinguished editor of *Finanz Archiv*, published in 1896 what was, and still is, a surprisingly original and challenging article, in which he proposed this definition: "Der Begriff [Einkommen] erweist sich als Reinvermögenszugang eines bestimmten Zeitabschnitts inkl. der Nutzungen und geldwerten Leistungen Dritter."[2] Two other

---

[1] G. Schmoller, "Die Lehre vom Einkommen in ihrem Zusammenhang mit den Grundprinzipien der Steuerlehre," *Zeitschrift für die gesamte Staatswissenschaft*, Vol. XIX (1863).

[2] "Der Einkommenbegriff und die Einkommensteuergesetze," *Finanz Archiv*, XIII (1896), 23. This article and Schanz's extended review (*Finanz Archiv*, XXXIX [1921], 505–23) of Bauckner's *Der privatwirtschaftliche Einkommenbegriff* constitute the most important contribution which has been made to the literature of our general subject. For similar definitions, following Schanz, see von Pistorius, *Unser Steuerrecht* (Stuttgart, 1929), II, 58–66; B. Moll, *Probleme der Finanzwissenschaft* (Leipzig, 1924), chaps. xii–xvi; Bauckner, *Der privatwirtschaftliche Einkommenbegriff* (München, 1921); J. Popitz, "Einkommensteuer," in *Handwörterbuch der Staatswissenschaft* (4th

passages from this article may be quoted to supplement this statement:

Wir wollen wissen, welche selbständige wirtschaftliche Kraft eine Person in einer bestimmten Periode darstellt, wollen wissen, welche Mittel sie in dieser Zeit zu ihrer Disposition hat, ohne dass sie ihr eigenes Vermögen verzehrt oder fremde Mittel (Schulden) hinzunimmt.[3]

Wir rechnen also zum Einkommen alle Reinerträge und Nutzungen, geldwerte Leistungen Dritter, alle Geschenke, Erbschaften, Legate, Lotteriegewinne, Versicherungskapitalen, Versicherungsrenten, Konjuncturengewinne jeder Art, wir rechnen ab alle Schuldzinsen und Vermögensverluste.[4]

Similar in content is Haig's conception, which he defines in these words: "Income is the money value of the net accretion to one's economic power between two points in time."[5] This may be taken as original with Haig, in view of his meager reference to the German literature. The conception lacks definiteness, as compared to that of Schanz, for Haig does not go far to describe its content in relation to particular problems of income determination. Even gifts he includes tentatively and with diffidence.[6]

While concurring entirely with the position of these

---

ed.); Strutz, *Kommentar zum Reichseinkommensteuer*, I, Introduction, 13 ff.; Vogel, *Finanz Archiv*, 1910, Band II, pp. 99 ff.; and Covero, *Bewertung der Vermögensgegenstande* (1912), pp. 137 ff. Unfavorable criticism of the Schanzian position has been indulged by most other prominent German writers in *Nationalökonomie* and *Finanzwissenschaft*, notably by Philippovich (see below, p. 68).

[3] Schanz, *op. cit.*, p. 5.

[4] *Ibid.*, p. 24.

[5] R. M. Haig, "The Concept of Income," in *The Federal Income Tax*, ed. R. M. Haig (New York, 1921), chap. i.

[6] *Ibid.*, p. 26.

writers, one may feel that their language is somewhat lacking in clarity and precision. Haig's definition, literally construed, would exclude consumption—which he clearly does not himself intend. Besides, economic power itself presents a rather formidable problem of definition. With Schanz, the reliance on *Reinvermögenszuwachs* (or *-zugang*) hardly avoids confusion. If one construes *Vermögen* broadly, generically, income is reduced merely to a sort of synonym for capacity or ability; while narrow construction would seem to identify income with accumulation. However, both of these definitions do carry the essential implication that income is a mere value fact; that the things to be valued—if one may be permitted such language—are rights; and that the idea of gain is fundamental. They would hardly object to a definition of income in terms of consumption and of property values at given points in time. Much seems to be gained by describing the concept in this manner, for from such definition one proceeds most easily to the actual task of measurement.

The extensive German controversy over *Einkommenbegriff* was waged most actively in the formative period of German income taxes. That less attention has been given to the subject since that time may be due in some measure to Schanz's devastating criticism of the narrower conceptions; but more important surely is the fact that the problem of policy was settled by the Prussian legislation of 1891 in a manner entirely satisfactory to the conservatives. The narrower conceptions prevailed, and Schanz appears to have had little success in initiating a movement for reform. His work did finally bear fruit in the *Reichseinkommensteuer*—though the broad definition of the Act of 1921 has been largely whittled away by subsequent legislation. This revival of the question as a political issue has led to some rejuvenation of the old controversy; and Schanz has now an important following.[7]

Most discussions of *Einkommenbegriff* begin at least with reference to Hermann. His most frequently quoted statement is this:

Dieses (Einkommen) ist vielmehr die Summe der wirtschaftlichen oder Tauschgüter, welche in einer gewissen Zeit zu dem ungeschmälert fortbestehenden Stammgut einer Person neu hinzutreten, die sie daher beliebig verwenden kann.[8]

This definition, of course, is essentially that of Adam Smith,[9] Malthus,[10] Rau, Schmoller, Sax, Mithoff, Mangoldt, and many others.[11] In interpreting his position, however, it is very important to recognize that

[7] See above, n. 2.

[8] *Staatswissenschaftliche Untersuchungen* (2d [posthumous] ed.; München, 1870), p. 582. Neumann observes that Hermann first says *verwenden darf* and then shifts (unfortunately, says Neumann) to *verwenden kann* (Neumann, *Grundlagen der Volkswirtschaftlehre* [Tübingen, 1899], p. 221, n. 222). Hermann later shifts back to *verwenden darf* (p. 594); but the context prohibits one's inferring that he regarded this as the more accurate language.

[9] Adam Smith, *Wealth of Nations*, Book II, chap. ii, sec. 5: "The gross revenue of all the inhabitants of a great country comprehends the whole annual produce of their land and labor; the net revenue, what remains free to them after deducting the expense of maintaining, first, their fixed, and, second, their circulating capital; or what without encroaching on their capital they can place in their stock reserved for immediate consumption, or spend upon their subsistence, conveniences, and amusements."

[10] Malthus, *Definitions in Political Economy:* "Revenue: That portion of the stock or wealth, which the possessor may annually consume without injury to his permanent resources."

[11] For citations to other German treatises see Schanz, *op. cit.;* also Robert Meyer, *Das Wesen des Einkommens* (Berlin, 1887), chap. i.

Hermann, like most early writers, is focusing attention upon the idea of social income and is only incidentally concerned with income from the point of view of individuals. This is clear at the very beginning of his discussion, when he says:

Neue Güter kann der Einzelne auch ohne wirtschaftliche Vergeltung von Andern erhalten; da dies aber eine blose Aenderung in der Verteilung, keine Vermehrung des Gesammteinkommens der Nation ist, so können wir hiervon absehen.[12]

This rather commonplace conception is usually referred to in the German literature as the *Konsumtionsfondstheorie*. It is, of course, something quite different from the Fisher conception, for the *Konsumtionsfond* is always delimited by the requirement of preserving intact the original capital. Such language seems hopelessly confusing; for what one *verzehren darf* or *verzehren kann*, while just maintaining intact one's initial capital, is rarely or never the same as what one actually *verzehrt*. If income is what one may consume without encroaching upon one's original capital, then it is merely a value fact and not a sum of goods or of consumption goods values. It is either consumption or not consumption; and, if it is consumption, one must, with Fisher, go the whole way. *Konsumtionsfondstheorie* appears to insist that income is consumption; but it insists equally on the proviso that consumption be not larger than something else.[13] If accretion of capital is not income, then impairment of capital is not a proper deduction.

[12] *Op. cit.*, p. 583.

[13] The criticism implied here is essentially the same as that advanced below against the "realization" criterion and Seligman's "separation." Incidentally, this emphasis upon consumption, at once the great error and the

These *Konsumtionsfondstheorien*, in general, display that absence of rigor and precision which so commonly characterizes definitions proposed with relation to no very special problem. Many of the writers seem only to be trying to indicate vaguely what sort of thing income is; and, among those already mentioned, several go on to impose important restrictions or qualifications. Most common is the requirement of *Regelmässigkeit.*

This requirement of regularity is essential to a variety of theories which the German literature, without clear distinctions, denotes as *Periodizitäts-, Quellen-,* and *Ertragskategorientheorien.* Gustav Cohn is a prominent proponent of the first variety of doctrine. He says: "Einkommen ist die Summe der Güter, welche in regelmässiger Wiederkehr einem Haushalte verfügbar wird."[14] Adolph Wagner is usually referred to as a representative of this view, although his language is often that of writers espousing the related doctrines. He con-

---

boasted contribution of most German writers, is often a mere superfluity. One suspects that it seemed important to them primarily because of their inability to grasp the underlying meaning of the "vom Standpunkte des capitalistischen Unternehmers berechneten Überschüsse."

To talk, with Hermann and others, of what one *verzehren darf*, implying that *man darf nicht das Kapital verzehren*, may seem, for some minds, to provide a grand simplification of a conception otherwise definable only in terms of value estimates. With all its inelegance, however, it really comes out just where our definition does, except for the possibility of endless controversy over precisely what *verzehrt werden darf!*

Schmoller himself proposes this definition: "[Einkommen ist] die Summe von Mitteln, welche der Einzelne, ohne in seinem Vermögen zurückzukommen, für sich und seine Familie, für seine geistigen und körperlichen Bedürfnisse, für seine Genüsse und Zwecke, kurz für Steigerung seiner Persönlichkeit in der Wirtschaftsperiode verwenden kann" (*op. cit.*, p. 52).

[14] *Grundlegung der Nationalökonomie* (1885), p. 211 (cited in Schanz, *op. cit.*, p. 12).

ceives income as a "Summe wirtschaftlicher Güter welche derselben in gewissen Perioden regelmässig und daher mit der Fähigkeit der regelmässigen Wiederholung als Reinerträge einer festen Erwerbsquelle neu als Vermögen hinzuwachsen."[15] He includes all income in kind and—what distinguishes him in an important way from other writers—also *regelmässige unentgeltliche Einnahme*. This, of course, indicates the essential role of recurrence in his conception. It is of more than passing interest that Wagner was not indisposed to admit non-recurrent receipts in the calculation of income for income taxation.[16]

Neumann, after criticizing other efforts to narrow the income concept, himself maintains that only receipts from permanent sources may properly be counted. He says:

Fortbauend auf jener älteren Charakteristik des Einkommens .... bezeichnen wir als Einkommen nicht die Einnahme, welche selber "fortdauernd," "wiederkehrend," oder gar "regelmässig wiederkehrend" erscheinen, aber doch diejenigen, welche die regelmässige, übliche Folge dauernder Bezugsquellen sind. Dann sind wir am Ziele.[17]

Neumann's formal definition is expressed as follows:

Der Inbegriff derjenigen Güter, geldwerten Leistungen (e.i. S) und Nutzungen fremder Dinge ist, welche als regelmässige Folge

[15] *Grundlegung der politischen Oekonomie* (3d ed., 1892), Part I, p. 405. On p. 407: "[Einkommen ist] der periodische sich regelmässig widerholende Reinertrag einer festen Erwerbsquelle, dessen Bezug einer Person rechtlich und thatsächlich zusteht, einschliesslich des Werthes der Genüsse und Genussmöglichkeiten aus dem Nutzvermögen dieser Person."

[16] "Praktisch wichtig wird das Alles besonders wieder für die Einkommensteuer. Hier wird man allerdings auch gewisse Kategorieen von Fällen nicht regelmässiger Einnahmen doch zum "Einkommen" in Sinn der Steuer rechnen müssen" (*ibid.*, p. 406).

[17] *Op. cit.*, p. 224.

dauernder Bezugsquelle, in gewisser Zeit Jemand der Art zuteil werden, dass er darüber in seinem Interesse verfügen kann.[18]

However, he does recognize the limitations of his own definition, saying:

Es bleibt hierbei manche Unsicherheit. . . . . Insbesonders kann nicht geleugnet werden, dass schon in jenen Worten "dauernde Bezugsquellen und regelmässige Folge" eine Unbestimmtheit liegt, die aus wissenschaftlicher Begriffs-bestimmung, wenn thunlich, verbannt werden sollte.[19]

Neumann is clearly intent from the beginning upon excluding gifts and bequests. His criticism of other writers relates not to the content of their conceptions but to the *Unsicherheit* of their language. He feels that his own definition provides a more useful and precise conception, avoids excluding items which common sense readily admits, and yet effectively excludes gratuities. One might infer that history has vindicated this view, for the *Quellentheorie* was incorporated in the Prussian income tax, inaugurated during the Michel reforms of the early nineties. Indeed, it is still retained, in form at least, in the *Reichseinkommensteuer*. But *Quellentheorie* is really much older. Neumann's definition seems to represent the result of deliberate effort merely to express in general terms the essential content of income as already defined for taxation, notably in the Prussian law of 1851. Like so many writers of the present day, he seems to have conceived the economist's task as merely that of showing how an economist would phrase definitions already fixed as to content in legislation.[20]

Neumann's definition is taken over without substan-

[18] *Ibid.*, p. 227.
[19] *Ibid.*, p. 226.   [20] *Ibid.*, pp. 225 ff.

tial change by Philippovich[21] and from him in turn, with perhaps some diffidence, by Schäffle.[22] Philippovich evidences surprising hostility to the Schanzian position. His almost scathing denunciation has exercised no small influence upon German thought; but its weight is merely that of an *ex cathedra* judgment of one who has preferred to rely upon his own prestige rather than upon the cogency of his argument. Commenting upon the *fiscalische Einkommentheorie*, he says:

> Damit hat Schanz nicht einen neuen Einkommensbegriff gewonnen oder einen älteren vervollkommnet, sondern den Begriff Einkommen überhaupt aus der menschlichen Wirtschaft eliminiert. Er kehrt damit zur Auffassung des Mittelalters zurück, die nur das Vermögen kennt.[23]

Fuisting, the author of the definitive *Kommentaren* on the Prussian income tax, is another outstanding and ardent proponent of *Quellentheorie*.[24]

The so-called *Ertragskategorientheorien* are not to be distinguished clearly from the *Periodizitäts-* or *Quellentheorien*, nor do they represent a class marked by any distinct common element. The name, however, is commonly applied to several doctrines, largely but not entirely similar to those already considered.

Many writers insist that income must arise from economic activity. To quote from Roscher:

> Der Begriff Einnahme umfasst alle Güter, die innerhalb einer gewissen Periode neu ins Vermögen treten, also auch durch

---

[21] *Allgemeine Volkswirtschaftlehre* (12th ed.), pp. 337–40, esp. p. 339.

[22] *Die Steuern*, p. 161.

[23] Philoppovich, *op. cit.*, p. 339.

[24] *Die Einkommensbesteuerung der Zukunft* (Berlin, 1903), II, Sec. A, esp. pp. 19–57.

Geschenk, Lotteriegewinn, Erbschaft, etc., Einkommen dagegen nur solche Einnahme, die aus einer wirtschaftlichen Tätigkeit hervorgehen.[25]

Vocke's emphasis is similar:

Einkommen [ist] das, was dem Wirtschafter nach Ersetzung der verwendeten Vermögensteile und Befriedigung der sich an seiner Wirtschaftsführung knüpfenden Rechtsansprüche und nach Abzug der Vermögensvermehrung durch blossen Vermögensübergang zur eigenen Verwendung übrig bleibt.[26]

Commenting on this statement, Schanz stresses the fundamental point when he says: "Vocke führt des Näheren aus, dass das Einkommen als Ganzes nur aus Ertrag bestehe, was nicht Ertrag sei, könne nicht Einkommen sein und umgekehrt."[27] Vocke argues for a sort of thoroughgoing yield conception; also, perhaps, for one which makes social income the primary concept. His view thus stands in clear opposition to those in which the essentially personal nature of income is fundamental.

As Popitz has observed,[28] Roscher's language would seem to exclude items like rents (he says *Renten und Unterstützungen*); and Lexis, perhaps the leading advocate of this sort of doctrine, appears to be endeavoring to avoid this unwanted implication when he substitutes *Wirtschaftsführung des Inhabers* for *wirtschaftliche Tätigkeit*. Lexis says:

Die als Einkommenteile verfügbar werdenden Güter müssen in innerem Zusammenhange mit der Wirtschaftsführung des

[25] *Grundlagen der Nationaölkonomie*, §§ 144 and 145.

[26] *Die Grundzüge der Finanzwissenschaft* (Leipzig, 1894), pp. 278 ff.

[27] *Op. cit.*, p. 10. Incidentally, our indebtedness to Schanz, throughout the first part of this chapter, is considerable.

[28] *Op. cit.*, p. 414.

Inhabers stehen. In der Regel sind sie Erträge seiner Arbeit oder seines Vermögens; immer aber, selbst in dem Falle eines Almosenempfängers, handelt es sich um Einnahme auf die die Wirtschaft vermöge ihrer besonderen Natur angewiesen ist.[29]

This, for Lexis, provides an adequate basis for excluding gifts, bequests, and lottery winnings. Incidentally, he condemns unreservedly the *Regelmässigkeit* criterion, saying, "der Einkommenbegriff (einschliesst) keineswegs Stetigkeit und regelmässige Wiederkehr der als Einkommen anzusehenden Einnahme."[30]

An interesting variant of this sort of definition is presented by Held in his early work:

Einkommen ist alles, was man rechtlicher Weise verzehren kann, ohne nach dem Verbrauch eine tauschwerte Erwerbsquelle (Kapital) und damit eine Gelegenheit des Erwerbs verloren zu haben, die man vorher hatte—alles was man rechtlicher und solider Weise verzehren kann.[31]

In the next chapter, "Näheres über den Einkommenbegriff"—a tedious and rather fruitless discussion—Held proceeds quite unencumbered by his original definition; and later, in the second edition of his *Grundriss*, he falls back on a simpler statement: "Einkommen ist, was ohne dauernde Vermögensminderung verzehrt und genossen werden kann."[32] To say this, is to incorporate

[29] "Einkommen," in *Wörterbuch der Volkswirtschaft* (2d ed., 1906), pp. 693 ff.

[30] *Ibid.*, p. 694.

[31] *Die Einkommensteuer* (Bonn, 1872), p. 54. This definition was approved by Burkhart, *Hirths Annalen* (1876), p. 58 (latter reference from Neumann, *op. cit.*, p. 220).

[32] *Grundriss für Vorlesungen über Nationalökonomie* (2d ed.; Bonn, 1872), p. 68: "Das Gesammteinkommen besteht aus derjenigen Quantität von innerhalb einer Zeitperiode neu entstehenden wirtschaftlichen Gütern,

candidly in one's definition the argument so often advanced in favor of *Periodizitäts-* and *Quellentheorien.* Thus, income is defined merely as an upper limit which consumption ought not to exceed. This is essentially the position taken more explicitly by Gerloff, after sharply adverse criticism of *Periodizitäts-* and *Quellentheorien.* He says:

> Einkommen [ist] die Wertsumme der einer Haushaltwirtschaft innerhalb einer Wirtschaftsperiode zufliessenden Erträge ihrer Erwerbswirtschaft und erwerbswirtschaftlichen Handlungen einschliesslich sonstiger geldwerter Bezüge und Nutzungen, die als planmässige Mittel der Bedarfsbefriedigung zu dienen bestimmt sind.[33]

His point is merely that *Vermögensveränderung und Eigentumsübertragungen* are not *Mittel planmässiger Bedarfsbefriedigung.*[34]

Walther Lotz entertains opinions regarding *Einkommenbegriff* which are interesting at least as curiosities. First, he endeavors to contribute his mite to the dialectical campaign against dangerous developments in

---

welche verzehrt werden kann, so dass am Ende ebensoviel Kapitalgüter vorhanden sind, wie am Anfang der Periode. Dazu kommt der Genuss des (erhaltenen) Nutzkapitals. Kürzer:—Einkommen ist, was ohne dauernde Vermögensverminderung verzehrt und genossen werden kann."

Two other statements may be quoted from the same chapter (p. 71): "Das Einzeleinkommen besteht aus dem Inhalt von Vermögensrechten (Waaren), das Gesammteinkommen aus Gütern. . . . . Die Grösse eines Einzeleinkommens ist gleich dem Werth des Inhalts der Vermögensrechte des Einzelnen an den das Gesammteinkommen ausmachenden Gütern resp. Nutzungen."

[33] "Grundlegung der Finanzwissenschaft," in *Handbuch der Finanzwissenschaft* (Tübingen, 1926), I, 44 ff., esp. p. 50.

[34] For excellent and devastating criticism of this sort of position one need only refer back to Neumann, *op. cit.,* pp. 221 ff.

the income tax. He recognizes weakness in the familiar definitions but says: "Der Grundgedanke, der in der Definition des Einkommens als Geldwert von Reinerträgen aus dauernden Bezugsquellen liegt, dürfte nicht unbedingt zu verwerfen sein."[35] He then proceeds to erect new foundations for a conception which he regards as derived from Philippovich. The argument may be digested as follows:

Taxes must in the long run be derived from the net annual production. Individuals may acquire goods through gambling, speculation, gifts, and bequests; but these individual gains contribute nothing to that reservoir from which all taxes must be drawn.

Die Volkswirtschaft liefert nur mehr an Mittel für Steuern, wenn die Production erfolgreich gesteigert worden ist und wenn bei bestehender Geldwirtschaft mehr Geldwerte an Gütern, Nutzungen und Diensten verfügbar geworden sind, als an Kosten aufgewandt worden ist.[36]

Taxes may not exceed, or indeed even equal, this amount, otherwise there would not be the means for capital maintenance or the incentive for accumulation.

The paragraph following upon these observations then begins as follows:

Einkommen als Grundlage der Besteuerung kann demnach [!] nur ergeben: das Mehr in Geld oder Geldwert, welches einzelnen Wirtschaftern oder Haushaltsgemeinschaften auf Grund von Productionstätigkeit nach Deckung der Productionskosten zufliesst. In anderen Worten sagt dasselbe Philippovich. . . . .[37]

Professor Lotz, of course, is a rarely conservative person; but it is amazing that his disapproval of certain

[35] *Finanzwissenschaft* (Tübingen, 1917), p. 445.

[36] *Ibid.*, p. 446.   [37] *Ibid.*, p. 446.

practices in the taxation of income should have led him into such outlandish sophistry. He has surely read Ricardo.[38] Surely, too, he has forgotten something from Schmoller:

Ist wirklich der fiktive Theil des National-Einkommens, aus welchem die Steuern gezahlt werden, notwendig auch der arithmetische Maasstab, nach welchem sie umzulegen sind. . . . . Nach unserer Ansicht ist die Bejahung dieser Frage einer der grössten logischen Sprunge, die je gemacht worden sind, ...[39]

At all events, one wonders what would happen if Professor Lotz were to carry this line of argument into discussion of taxes other than those upon income.

Lotz's conception of labor income involves another rather unique contribution. Here he perverts the concept of income in a good cause; and it seems ungenerous to criticize so conservative a scholar for assertions with genuinely liberal implications. His contention is that modern income taxes are inconsistent in not providing adequate production-cost deductions in the case of personal-service incomes. His argument is relevant and cogent with reference to the case for differentiation; but what becomes of the concept of income if one follows Lotz:

Productionskosten des Arbeitseinkommens sind unbedingt die Kosten des Lebensunterhaltes des Arbeitenden und seiner Familie, daneben noch Rücklagen für den Fall der Arbeitsunfähigkeit, ausserdem, sofern es sich nicht um lebenslänglich angestellten Beamten handelt, Rücklagen für den Fall der Arbeitslosigkeit. Hierzu treten Kosten der Verzinsung und Amortisation des Erziehungs- und Ausbildungskapitales, Fürsorge für die Hinterbleibenen und für die Kosten des Begräb-

38 *Principles*, chap. viii. 39 *Op. cit.*, p. 32.

nisses, ferner, soweit nicht ein Ruhegehaltssystem herrscht, Rücklagen für die unproduktive Altersperiode, endlich die Auslagen für Anschaffung von Arbeitsmaterial und Arbeitsräumen, soweit nicht ein Arbeitsgeber dem Arbeitenden solche stellt, endlich die Fahrtkosten von und zur Arbeitsstätte.[40]

Many of these deductions would be necessary in order to place recipients of personal-service incomes on a parity with those living from property. Even from this point of view, however, Lotz goes much too far. One may, with Schanz,[41] inquire whether laborers live in order to work or work in order to live! It is necessary to distinguish between consumption and expense; one cannot include particular outlays under both heads. Furthermore, this is simply not a world in which laborers are dealt in and valued as property. While this imposes limitations on the income concept, for some purposes, it is presumably best to recognize and accept these limitations, instead of destroying the concept in trying to remove them.

Along with these German definitions one may mention one that has been espoused in this country. Professor Plehn, in his presidential address to the American Economic Association,[42] explained that income was

[40] *Op. cit.*, p. 449. It is interesting that, in the recent (1931) edition of this work, Professor Lotz has omitted the whole section from which this and the foregoing quotations were taken. In the revised edition, the author's discussion of *Einkommenbegriff* is confined to brief comment, in connection with German income-tax practice, on the position of Schanz, with no adverse criticism of that position (see Lotz, *Finanzwissenschaft* [2d ed.; Tübingen, 1931], pp. 490–94).

[41] *Finanz Archiv*, XXXIX (1921), 408–11 (II, 110–13).

[42] C. C. Plehn, "The Concept of Income as Recurrent, Consumable Receipts," *American Economic Review*, XIV (1924), 1–12. There are no references to foreign literature.

merely "recurrent, consumable receipts." Such language invites severe criticism. It is hardly more appropriate to think of income as receipts than to regard the balance-sheet account, surplus, as represented by cash. That income must be consumable can mean almost nothing unless it mean "consumable without impairment of capital"; and impairment of capital cannot be defined consistently without repudiation of the receipts conception. Furthermore, Plehn's phraseology, although the author does not mention its antecedents, really goes back at least as far as Hermann and has been commonplace abroad for over a century. To be sure, it has been somewhat out of fashion in Germany since the eighties; but it still finds occasional expression in current literature. Definitions almost identical with that of Professor Plehn are also to be found in the standard French treatises on income tax.[43]

Meticulous criticism of these narrower conceptions of income perhaps would not be in good proportion here. Besides, the job was done quite thoroughly by Schanz in 1896. Bauckner presumably has essayed much the same task in his *Der privatwirtschaftliche Einkommenbegriff*, though his work seems open to serious criticism at those points where he departs from Schanz. Briefer criticism of the same order, and of excellent quality, is advanced by Bruno Moll in his *Probleme der Finanzwissenschaft*,[44] and by J. Popitz in an admirable article on *Einkommen-*

[43] E.g., Allix et Lecercle, *L'Impôt sur le revenu* (Paris, 1926), Vol. I, chap. viii, esp. pp. 166–70.

[44] See also his more recent (but not better) *Lehrbuch der Finanzwissenschaft* (Berlin, 1930), pp. 458–87.

steuer in the recent edition of the *Handwörterbuch der Staatswissenschaft*. Our own comments will be confined to criticism of a rather general nature.

Let us note, in the first place, the fundamental similarity of all the definitions to which we have referred. They agree surprisingly as to the specific items which should be excluded in the calculation of income; and differences among them reflect variety of opinion as to what arrangement of verbal symbols would at once describe a workable concept and still not admit too much. The criterion of *Regelmässigkeit* was obviously inadequate.[45] It could not be strictly construed; and, marginal cases apart, it led clearly to exclusion of items commonly acknowledged to be admissible. So, for Neumann and others, the emphasis upon the idea of an enduring source seemed at least somewhat preferable. But no proponent of *Quellentheorien* really undertook to define *Quelle*. As Bruno Moll observes:

> Statt des Einkommenbegriffs ist nunmehr der Quellenbegriff das zu definierende Etwas. Eine befriedigende, eindeutige, klar abgegrenzte Definition der Quelle finden wir nirgends, ja sie würde nicht einmal versucht.[46]

Neumann and his followers, indeed, often come perilously near to the confession that the test of the existence of a source may often be the presence of recurring, if perhaps fluctuating, revenue. Gerloff's *Mittel der planmässigen Bedarfsbefriedigung* is obviously so near to *Erträge mit der Fähigkeit der Wiederkehr* that the improvement upon, and escape from, what Gerloff himself

[45] See esp. Neumann, *op. cit.*, and Lexis, *op. cit.*

[46] *Probleme der Finanzwissenschaft*, p. 127.

roundly condemns does little credit to a person of his competence.

The requirement that income must arise from *wirtschaftliche Tätigkeit*, or must be connected with the *Wirtschaftführung des Inhabers*, may be viewed as but another means of imposing the same criterion. Most recurring revenue would be included, and most non-recurring items left out. However, this view is often espoused by writers who have no immediate concern about the definition of personal income as such. Lexis, for example, is interested in income as a concept for theory; and he appears merely to be seeking a definition of personal income such that summation will afford the most useful conception of social income. Other writers begin by defining social income as a summation of individual incomes and then proceed to inquire how personal income may best be defined in order to make the summation most significant.[47] Such approach, as we have already suggested, is hardly compatible with the best definition of personal income.

Against all these doctrines one must urge, as a perhaps decisively important point, that there is something eminently personal about income. This is emphasized by the Germans in their distinctions between *Einkommen* and *Ertrag*.[48] They stress the subjective character of the former (*subjectiv*, of course, is not "psychic")

[47] For discussion typical in this respect see E. Schuster, "Einkommen und Volkseinkommen," *Schriften des Vereins für Sozialpolitik*, CLXXIII, Teil I, 55-97.

[48] See, e.g., von Heckel, "Einkommensteuer," in *Wörterbuch der Volkswirtschaft* (2d ed., 1906), p. 699; Schuster, *op. cit.*, and almost any standard treatise on economics or public finance.

and the association of *Ertrag* with things rather than persons. All this is usually forgotten, however, when they come actually to the task of definition, for they exhibit *Einkommen* merely as a sort of *Bündel* of *Erträge* —to employ a happy phrase from the incisive criticism of Popitz.[49]

The confusion arises largely from the manner in which the problem is stated. Most discussion appears to be directed toward answering the question: What kind of items are income and what kind, not-income? At the risk of seeming pedantic, one may insist that inquiry is more properly addressed to a different problem: How should the calculation of income proceed? Income is merely the result of certain arithmetical operations; and confusion is inescapable as soon as one attempts to classify receipts into income and not-income. Bruno Moll is one who has seen this quite clearly:

> Das Einkommen ist also erst das Ergebnis einer Rechnung. Es lässt sich von der Einnahme, die über der Schwelle der Einzelwirtschaft tritt, nicht von vornherein oder in diesem Augenblick sagen: Sie ist Einkommen oder ist es nicht.[50]

One may also recall the words of Schäffle: "Das Einkommen hat nur buchhalterische Existenz."[51]

If the essential feature of income is gain, then personal income cannot be defined apart from the circum-

---

[49] *Op. cit.*, p. 415. He says: "der Einkommenbegriff verliert damit an Eigenart, das Einkommen wird zu einem Bündel der Quellenerträge. . . . ."

[50] *Probleme der Finanzwissenschaft*, p. 132.

[51] See above, chap. ii, p. 51, n. 13. One may note also the opposite bias in Meyer (*Das Wesen des Einkommens*, p. 19): "sie [the accounting approach] droht trotz Schmollers Verwahrung dem Einkommen den Charakter des 'lebendigen Ganzen' zu rauben, und das Einkommen zu einem 'wirtschaftlichen Rechnungs-exempel' zu machen."

stances of individuals. One may insist—as do most writers, in fact—that the yields of various revenue sources merely converge upon a person and constitute his income. Conceding that this is not unintelligible, one may still emphasize the fact that the proper deductions cannot be ascertained so long as one looks merely to these revenues and their sources. Certainly there is something peculiarly personal about expense. The gain to an individual during a period from ownership of given property depends not merely upon the rental return, repair expense, taxes, and similar things having to do with the property itself, but also upon the terms under which he acquired and held that property.[52] Indeed, as we have already pointed out, the separation between expense and consumption leads ultimately to a question of personal motive or intention.

The quite arbitrary character of the criterion of recurrence hardly merits further comment. However, let us remember that, while yields or receipts may appropriately—if not rigorously—be classified as recurrent and nonrecurrent, such characterization of gains is dangerous. Gain is an abstraction which we should take care not to hypostatize. It is something which has to do fundamentally with persons, not with things. Gain contributes to the economic power of a person or group and is the net result of his (their) relation with the market or community. Income, to repeat, is merely the end re-

---

[52] This may be illustated by the case of stockholders in a corporation which declares an extraordinary dividend "from surplus." The corporation is, so to speak, distributing earnings. However, it seems clear that the income position of individuals as shareholders depends in each case upon the terms on which, and the time when, they became shareholders.

sult of arithmetic operations with value facts. While these calculations may, in some circumstances, lead to results which vary little from period to period, it is best to confine our characterization of recurrence to things coming in and things going out.

We turn now to brief consideration of the familiar criterion of realization. A standard manual on our federal income tax quotes Professor Haig's definition of income and then remarks: "It should include the word realized"[53]—as though the omission were only a careless oversight! This view is widely held by accountants, by the courts, and even by some economists. It derives clearly enough from the conventional practices of financial accounting. The accountant, faced with problems of valuation for which data are often meager, has developed and followed religiously a rule-of-thumb procedure which sacrifices relevance to "accuracy." Instead of attempting the best estimates which can be made, he is usually content to employ figures already available in his accounts and thus to minimize demands upon mere judgment.[54]

His methods appear to be founded upon profound

[53] Montgomery, *Income Tax Procedure* (New York, 1926), p. 590. One wonders how Haig may react to his colleague's proposal to destroy his definition by introducing an innocent little participle. Likewise, one might wish to know with what feeling Schanz may have read Max Lion's essay in the volume dedicated to Schanz (*Beiträge zur Finanzwissenschaft* [Tübingen 1928], II, 273–300). Lion, a specialist in *Bilanzsteuerrecht*, finds that Schanz is not clearly free from the careless error which Montgomery has noted in Haig!

[54] One might say that he often eschews valuation entirely. At least, one finds difficulty in the idea that an inventory is being "valued" when different parts of an inventory of identical goods are priced differently—as is approved practice.

mistrust of both his professional colleagues and his em-
ployers. The reputable accountant never loses sight of
the fact that his income statements are influential in
matters of dividend policy. Income, for him, is perhaps
only what may be reported safely to unsophisticated
directors as income. He aims, it would seem, never to
ascertain what income is, in any really definable sense,
but rather to devise rules of calculation which will make
the result a minimum or at least give large answers only
in the future. Conventional accounting, moreover, not
only employs a procedure with a markedly conservative
bias but promptly repudiates this procedure whenever it
shows signs of working the other way. When prices
drawn from actual transactions on his books afford excessive estimates, the accountant promptly appeals to
the market for his valuations.

That such worship of conservatism—and professional
conspiracy against truth—is an unmixed evil, in a
world of corruptible accountants and optimistic directors, one may hesitate to assert. Where such rule-of-
thumb procedure is so universal, however, there is undue
resistance to departure from it where different methods
are clearly desirable. Furthermore, there is in many
quarters a disposition to maintain that methods of calculation deemed expedient in business indicate exhaus-
tively the real meaning of income. It is easy for most
people to elevate rules-of-thumb into logical necessities;
and persons do seriously maintain, with more than verbal paradox, that income not realized is not income.[55]

[55] Just as many Germans, after declaring that gratuitous receipts are not
income, later classify and discuss these same items as *abgeleitetes Einkommen*.

Our comments need imply no criticism of the accountant's practical wisdom; yet one may lament the effects of his practice and preaching upon unwary minds, especially in a world where courts insist upon investing somewhat technical terms with their connotations in everyday usage.[56]

Advocates of the recurrence criterion have undertaken to construct a concept of personal income from that of productivity or yield from things. Those who emphasize realization are attempting to define personal income in terms of transaction profit. In either case, it simply cannot be done. If all business ventures were initiated and completed within the fiscal period, the realization criterion would lead to no serious confusion. But, in a world where ventures often have neither beginning nor end within the lives of interested parties, it is hard to argue that one may grow richer indefinitely without increasing one's income.[57] Furthermore, since transaction income implies no imputation to preassigned periods of

[56] It is only fair to say that many reputable accountants would hesitate to maintain that their revenue figures measure income. Their task is that of reaching significant revenue results—significant for current dividend policy and for period-to-period comparisons. So, they may charge or credit items directly to balance-sheet accounts without implication that these items are unrelated to income or to what should be reached under an income tax. To say that current revenue figures would be impaired by inclusion of gains or losses not really attributable to this period is not to say that such gains or losses have nothing to do with income. However, the accountant seems a bit unfaithful to the realization criterion whenever he talks about income's being attributable to previous periods. For enlightened discussion along these general lines, see W. A. Paton, *Accounting* (New York, 1924), esp. chaps. xxv and xxvii.

[57] "From a practical common-sense point of view, there is something strange in the idea that a man may indefinitely grow richer without ever

time, how may one develop from it a conception wherein such imputation is fundamental?

The emphasis of accounting upon the transaction of sale would be fairly appropriate for merely merchandising enterprises, if only prices were extremely stable.[58] It is always more appropriate to merchandising than to manufacture and, in general, is least expedient for enterprises where the selling function is least important. But surely no adequate conception of annual, personal income can be built around the notion of transaction profit. To be sure, one never knows the final result of a business venture until it is completed. But the whole notion of accrual must be abandoned if one adheres rigorously to the test of realization. The argument that recognition of appreciation involves "anticipation of profit" which may never be obtained, fails to recognize the fundamental continuity of economic relations and ignores the essential value implications of income.

If an individual purchases one share of stock for $100 on January 1 and, on December 31, another share of the same stock for $150, the realization criterion demands that his income for the year be calculated by valuing one share at $100 and the other at $150. Here, it is surely as reasonable to argue that he may never realize

---

being subject to an income tax" (T. R. Powell, *Harvard Law Review*, XXXV, 376).

Incidentally, the theory of accounting regards the enterprise as perpetual. However appropriate this fiction may be in some uses, it can hardly be carried over bodily in a tax which applies to natural persons without unfortunate results.

[58] One may speculate with some amusement upon the results of traditional procedures of inventory valuation, say, in Germany, during the inflation.

$150 from the second share as that he may never realize the gain on the first. Suppose a man buys a Liberty Bond on January 1 for $90 and that on December 31 such bonds are selling for $100. He has "realized" no income. However, if he sells the bond at the latter date and puts the proceeds into unmarketable stock of a company prospecting for gold on Manhattan Island, he has "realized" income of $10. If he had merely traded the shares, and if the one acquired had no definite market value, a plenary session of the casuists would be necessary to pass on the case![59]

The realization criterion also leads to the same sort of confusion as that which arises from the attempt to define *Einkommen* in terms of *Ertrag*. One realizes on assets; one converts assets from one form into another; and one may "realize" cash, potatoes, or chicken pox. But gain simply is not something which may be delivered at one's doorstep. One may gain without realizing and realize without gaining; and, if either is essential to the existence of income, the other must be excluded. Common sense and established usage suggest that gain is the true *sine qua non;* but much of the current discussion of the income concept, especially by the courts, may be regarded as emphasizing realization to the exclusion of gain. If a corporation has undistributed income, then distributions are treated as income to shareholders on that evidence alone. Extraordinary dividends "from surplus" are taxable as income to all shareholders alike, even if they have acquired stock shortly

[59] For very effective discussion of the anomalies of "realization" see Paton, *op. cit.*, p. 624.

before, at prices which fully discount the dividend forth-coming.[60]

In emphasis upon the necessity of realization, Professor Seligman has outdone even the accountants.[61] Seeking to show how an economist would dispose of the stock-dividend problem—and his assistance evidently was not spurned by the Supreme Court—he proceeds to define income in such manner as to exclude stock dividends and then moves merrily to his conclusion. Professor Seligman's definition appears to be both original and unique; but he has evidently no misgivings as to the finality of his contribution, for he says:

> When income taxes were first introduced, economic science was only in its infancy and the above analysis of the relations between capital and income had not yet been worked out. We therefore find a considerable confusion. . . . .[62]

He begins by defining income as satisfactions. "Income is therefore fundamentally pleasure or benefit income."[63] On the next page, "Income denotes any inflow of satisfactions which can be parted with for money."[64] So far income would seem to be consumption. Before long, however, income becomes something more familiar —savings being slipped in quite unceremoniously. Per-

---

[60] Shareholders will be permitted deduction, of course, if the stock is sold subsequently at a loss; but, if a shareholder purchases before the dividend and dies shortly afterward (or at any time before disposing of the stock), no offset for the initially excessive tax is available. If he waits over a year, the value of the potential deduction may be greatly diminished by the capital-loss provisions.

[61] E. R. A. Seligman, "Are Stock Dividends Income?" *American Economic Review*, 1919, pp. 517–36.

[62] *Ibid.*, p. 527.

[63] *Ibid.*, p. 517.   [64] *Ibid.*, p. 518.

haps now we are dealing with realized and separated gain. But farther on we find that "in reality, capital or capital value is the result of income or income value."[65] So, income is now *Ertrag*, yield, or productivity. But on page 523 this, in turn, ceases to be true, for "in order to estimate the real net income from a piece of capital, we must therefore deduct from earnings the amount of the annual depreciation charge."[66] That is to say:

Income in the true sense of net income is that which is separated from the capital, while leaving the capital intact. As it has elsewhere been defined: Income as contrasted with capital denotes that amount of wealth which flows in during a definite period and which is at the disposal of the owner for purposes of consumption, so that in consuming it, his capital remains unimpaired.[67]

On page 518: "The quality of periodicity is essential." It is still so on page 521. But on page 528 it not only ceases to be essential but is excluded utterly: "Thus, the newer conception of income comprises not alone money, but money's worth; not alone regular, but irregular receipts; not alone gains from a usufruct, but gains from the disposal of the thing that yields the usufruct."[68] Incidentally, the author is to be congratulated for following his "realization" and "separation" to the bitter end of including not only capital gains but gifts and bequests as well.[69]

Seligman's differentiation between the growth of a herd and the growth of a forest is one of the less obscure features of his argument. "The increment in the value

[65] *Ibid.*, p. 521.

[66] *Ibid.*, p. 523.   [68] *Ibid.*, p. 528.

[67] *Ibid.*   [69] *Ibid.*

of a herd [from births] is income, because it is both real-ized and separated."[70] But of the growing forest he says:

> If, however, the trees are not cut, the forest becomes more valuable. . . . . What would have been income has been con-verted into capital increment. But this capital increment is not income because it is not separated and because it is not capable of separation if uncut. When the trees are ultimately cut, the gain undoubtedly becomes income. Up to that time, however, the increase in the value of the forest is only inchoate income.[71]

Thus, the gain, because not separated, becomes capital; yet the capital, in turn, becomes income when the sep-aration is finally effected. Income depends upon the number of trees cut—but only provided they do not cut too many! Certainly the phrase "inchoate income" de-serves prominent place among the curiosities of eco-nomic terminology.

After an extended parade of dogmatic assertions—put forward as necessities of logic—the author observes rather casually: "The reason why a mere unrealized in-crease in the value of land does not constitute income is primarily [sic] because of the uncertainty as to whether this particular consequence [a subsequent decline in value] may not happen."[72] Yet, later on, after arguing that any conversion of assets involves separation and realization, he asserts that "realization does not mean immunity from loss. Realization occurs when actual separation has been effected."[73] On the same page he speaks of "separation of earnings from the principal,"[74]

[70] *Ibid.*, p. 524.

[71] *Ibid.*

[72] *Ibid.*, p. 529.

[73] *Ibid.*, p. 536.

[74] *Ibid.*

in the case of a corporate dividend, as though this were an appropriate way to characterize a transfer of title to assets.

Professor Seligman's insistence both upon "realization" and upon depreciation deductions seems to involve serious logical difficulties. All credit items must be realized; but the requirements for admission on the debit side are much less exacting. Surely no definition of income which admits "mere value changes" only in one direction can well escape the fate of appearing ridiculous. Incidentally, Seligman leaves his reader in a state of some uncertainty as to what distinction was intended between realization and separation. He all but says explicitly that anything separated is realized; and the proposition seems quite obvious when the words are interchanged. Of course, it goes without saying that, after dragging in an amazing variety of income concepts and choosing useful attributes from different ones at will, Seligman finds little difficulty in throwing out an item like stock dividends, which was almost defenseless from the start.[75]

Realization, as requisite to the existence of income, may be retained, as already suggested, if one is willing to abandon the criterion of gain. It is only necessary logically that the two be not imposed together. Of course, if one were to follow Seligman, realization per se would denote merely something like total turnover. But it is possible to define realization in such manner as to

[75] Professor Seligman appears to derive his "realization" criterion from the consumption or psychic-income concept and his "separation" from the *Ertrag*, yield, or productivity conception—which further suggests the dangers inherent in Fisher's terminological tricks. See below, pp. 90 ff.

exclude mere conversion or exchange of assets. Realization, broadly conceived, is something achieved only in consumption, for only there does one find a stopping-place among the sequence of economic relations. Consumption is essentially a destruction, a using-up, an end. Such a solution of the dilemma, however, is not one that will commend itself to most advocates of the realization-criterion. Indeed, it finds almost a lone supporter—Professor Fisher, whose views we shall now consider.

Professor Fisher is the arch opponent of the kind of doctrine which we have espoused.[76] Our quarrel with him, however, Professor Fisher to the contrary notwithstanding, is essentially one of terminology rather than of logic. He recognizes clearly the income concept which we have tried to define and only inveighs against its being called income instead of earnings. Yet, since the quarrel is made out to be more than verbal, by Fisher and others, it will be necessary to indicate points at which issue may be joined. In passing, one may observe that Fisher's work is relatively free from the confused argument and indefinable language which characterize other proponents of narrower income concepts.

First of all, let us remember that Fisher's definition of income has its origin in analysis of the problem of capital and interest. For time-preference theory, value depends upon income; and proponents of this theory may hesitate to concede with us that income depends

[76] We shall undertake few footnote references to particular passages in Fisher's well-known treatises. His *Capital and Income* (New York, 1912) deals most specifically with the issues which concern us here. *The Theory of Interest* (New York, 1930), however, is of at least equal importance. Chap. ii of this later work contains an adequate summary of "Capital and Income."

upon value. This seeming paradox may be dissolved, either by recognizing that income has utterly different connotations in the two propositions or, waiving that, by straightening out certain misconceptions in the theory of interest itself.

It seems not unfair to say that Fisher is guilty of no little verbal legerdemain in his double usage of the income concept. Part of the time he is talking about income in the sense of values realized in consumption; but, whenever he is dealing with the valuation of capital goods, he uses income in exactly what we have defined as the yield, rent, or productivity sense. This confusion of language is the less pardonable because Fisher seems to have been well aware of what he was doing—though the confession is confined to a footnote.[77] What is discounted in the valuation of property is future yield (*Ertrag*), which may or may not be consumed. What are discounted are yields, not "consumptions."

Turning now to interest theory as such, one may say that time-preference theory permits of two interpretations. It may mean that the interest rate is determined by the prevailing rate at which future goods (yields, receipts) are discounted. This seems to assert merely that the rate of interest is determined by the rate of interest, for surely future goods are discounted at the market rate. On the other hand, the doctrine may be

[77] "The terms income and outgo are somewhat unfortunate, as, etymologically, they suggest the relation to the owner Smith rather than to its source, the farm. Smith's income is the farm's 'outcome' or yield (in German, *Ertrag*)" (*Capital and Income*, p. 122, n. 1).

For rather feeble apology for Fisher's double usage of the term see Canning, *Economics and Accountancy* (New York, 1929), p. 148, n. 1.

held to mean that the rate of interest depends upon the rate of saving—in which case it becomes orthodox classical doctine (in an especially untenable form). And in neither case is the problem especially illuminated.

Classical doctrine gives us a "cost theory"; and this can have no place in the description of equilibrium or in a discipline which must be strictly relativistic if rigorous. Saving, ultimately, is really a problem of demand, not of supply; and no significance can well be attached to the idea of an equilibrium rate of saving or an equilbrium supply of capital. Cost doctrines of interest are just as rigorous and just as illuminating as cost doctrines of wages, and no more so.

The phenomenon of interest must be regarded as arising primarily from the possibility of using resources to produce more and different resources. Interest theory properly is merely analysis of the factors governing rational demand for produced instruments. Indeed, it is not essential that interest be regarded as a separate price at all, though this may facilitate exposition. It may rather be conceived merely as a pervasive relation among certain prices or systems of prices.

The fundamental assumption is merely that new investment funds will pour into the more profitable employments. We may start with a situation where every instrument has a certain productivity or series of annual yields for the future, product prices remaining as they are. Likewise, every instrument has a certain cost, measured in terms of prices of resources necessary to its production. (Constant cost may be assumed for simplicity.) Now, knowing the prospective rental value of each instrument for each year in the future, at present product prices, and knowing its cost, we may compute the rate of interest at which these future yields will have a present value equal to the cost. When that rate is relatively high, the instrument will be produced rapidly, the output of industries using it will expand, and product prices will fall. Partly on account of this price change, and perhaps also because of change in the proportions of factors in production, the rental value or yield (value of differential product increments) of the instruments will fall. In cases where the imputed rate of interest is low, changes will be of the opposite character.[78]

In a progressive or changing world, forces will always be in operation toward ever changing equilibrium positions, as regards the allocation of investment. Careful description of the equilibrium condition is the very essence of interest theory. Resources used in production of new instruments must have the same productivity (value of differential product increment) and must command the same rental prices as like resources used in the making of consumption goods; and they must have the same productivity in the making of every kind of instrument. Moreover, the cost of instruments of every kind

[78] It has seemed appropriate, in this hasty digression, to disregard interest as a factor in the cost of producing instruments. To introduce it would practically require recourse to simple algebraic statement, ordinary literary statement of the relations being awkward and cumbersome. One might treat interest as a variable factor in cost and then solve for the rates simultaneously. Or, one might start from the technical beginnings, treating outlays during construction merely as negative receipts, and determining the rate of interest at which the total series of negative and positive receipts would discount to zero.

must be related to their respective future yields—calculated for each year with regard for their gradual deterioration, and assuming maintenance of current product prices—in such manner that the imputed rate is the same in each case. In other words, the present value of future rents must equal the cost at an interest rate which is the same in every instance. Thus, the cost of an instrument governs its value, even though that be also the discounted value of future yields, for those yields are themselves governed partly (though indirectly) by the cost of producing the instrument. In general, the rate of interest is determined by available opportunities for investment, given the rate at which funds are seeking investment or the amount of purchasing power reserved from consumption uses per interval of time.

To treat the cost of different instruments as variables in this problem will only somewhat complicate the exposition, provided one does not introduce cost functions incompatible with the assumption of competition. For some, the constant-cost assumption will seem an adequate approximation to the facts or, at least, an adequate basis for prescriptive theory. Persons accustomed to teach and think economics in terms of schedules, curves, and simultaneous equations will hasten on to treat the volume of savings itself as a function of the rate of interest. The equations may still be solved, perhaps, and the exercise may be agreeable; but humbler folk who are resigned to being merely economists may well inquire what is the problem of economy (what is being economized) in a system of theory which treats

the supplies (or the rate of change in supplies) of resources as functions of their prices. At all events, the
approach to interest theory which we have suggested
permits the building of a foundation independent of
supply considerations and thus relatively free from controversial elements. This done, one may proceed to
superimpose any or all types of supply functions which
may seem significant or amusing; or, one may confess
that he knows nothing about the supply side of the
problem and is not professionally concerned with phi-
losophies of history anyway.

This excursion into interest theory is intended to suggest, what should have been obvious from the start,
that there is no circularity in the position that value
determines income. Nor is one led into any logical im-
passe by defining terms in a manner different from that
of Professor Fisher. To dispose of the familiar paradox,
one may point out that the relation between income
(yield) and value, in the case of capital goods, is by no
means a one-way relation. The cost of instruments has
important consequences for their rate of production; and
the rate of production certainly affects their yield or
productivity. The statement that income (yield) determines or causes value is only a dangerous half-truth,
for income (yield) is not a datum in the problem. Certainly it is preposterous for Fisher to criticize another's
terminological system on the ground that it precludes
his making that statement,[79] especially when one re-

[79] Much of Fisher's criticism of other writers suggests that his own
terminological system has some foundation in the ultimate nature of things.
See, e.g., his criticism of Cannan (*Capital and Income*, pp. 247–49).

With respect to the merits of Fisher's whole conceptual setup, it is inter-

members his own confusing use of the word whose definition is at issue. In reply to all his preaching about
other people's use of language, we may maintain that
enormous confusion could be avoided if everyone would
simply quit talking about "discounting future incomes."
It would be a fair compromise, however, if everyone
took pains to avoid ambiguity as between income
from things (including human labor) and income *to*
persons.

Time-preference theories are also interesting for their
emphasis upon consumption as the unique end of all
economic behavior. The discounting process is conceived in terms of choices between present and future
consumption goods, as though all saving were intended
as redistribution of consumption through time. Now the
observable fact is that many people save instead of
consuming, just as some smoke pipes instead of cig-
arettes; and it seems reasonable to hold that the choices
are of the same order in the two cases. To assert that
considerations of utility determine the allocation of consumption funds explains nothing at all but merely says,
with egregious extravagance of language, that people
consume what they consume. Nor is there greater economy of language when one attempts to achieve another
dialectical triumph with the sword of utility by "explaining" the choices between consumption and accumulation. There is raised here a most difficult problem of

---

esting to note that his terminology precludes his treating interest as a cost.
This leaves his whole analysis without clear relevance to the problem of the
social economy of time or to the scarcity of loan funds as a factor in the allocation of resources among industries producing different consumption
goods.

social psychology and culture history;[80] and it hardly becomes the economist to make a pretense of competence by resort to verbal legerdemain. To assume that all economic behavior is motivated by desire for consumption goods, present and future, is to introduce a teleology which is both useless and false.[81]

Indeed, the whole distinction between consumption and saving may well be expressed in terms not of individual purpose but rather of social consequences of different employments of purchasing power. One tends to conserve and augment productive capacity; the other involves loss and destruction of economic goods. One person secures self-expression by increasing his wealth at a prodigious rate; another, by making his business the largest in the community; another, by providing the finest cultural opportunities for his children; another, by traveling the world over. Many people save mainly because it is the thing to do, because it is ex-

[80] One finds in the article of Schmoller's, to which we have already referred, a passage full of pointed implications. He says: "Damit wollen wir behaupten, dass nicht ein gerechtes Steuersystem, wie wir es auf Grundlage des Hermann'schen Einkommens als Verteilungsmaaszstab entwickeln werden, eine Stütze für das Nichtangreifen des Kapitals sein könne. Die wichtigste Garantie aber für Erhaltung desselben liegt in dem wirtschaftlichen Sinne, in dem sittlichen Geiste, in der ganzen Lebens und Kulturrichtung eines Volkes, in dem Umstande, dass ein Land überhaupt ökonomisch, politisch und moralisch vorwärts schreite" ("Die Lehre vom Einkommen . . . . , op. cit., p. 34).

[81] There is no reason, by the way, why rigorous interest theory should not be entirely applicable to a society where every increase in productive capacity was employed merely to increase productive capacity, the scale of consumption remaining constant indefinitely. In such a world, Messrs. Foster and Catchings would receive smaller royalties, and most of our texts in "Principles" would have to be considerably revised; and this would partially compensate for the strange perversion of tastes in the community.

pected of them. Certainly, the accumulation of property is often, if not typically, motivated by desires of the same order as those expressed in invidious consumption. In a world where capital accumulation proceeds as it does now, there is something sadly inadequate about the idea of saving as postponed consumption.

All this is perhaps relevant to the much argued question: Are savings income? Not only is it gratuitous, for our purposes, to divide goods into those yielding pleasurable sensations and those which are intermediate but, if these words mean anything at all, it seems hard to deny that acquisition of property rights may mean increase of power, greater freedom, security, prestige, and respectability. These are as much objectives of endeavor as are lapels on one's coat or diamonds on shirt fronts. Income implies achievement of certain objectives; and these achievements we propose to measure by the impartial judgment of the market. The market asserts that property rights are just property rights, whether they permit one's eating eggs or clipping coupons. Likewise, the market values additional resources just as it values vegetables; and the economic circumstances of him who owns either is measured in terms of prices or values. Why he may have bought claims to future goods, services, or funds, rather than that which he might eat or drink at the moment, the market does not inquire.

To ask whether savings are income suggests again the disposition to think of income in terms of things. Saving is accomplished by certain uses of purchasing power; savings are expenditure (if we disregard monetary disturbances of hoarding and dishoarding). Income is not saved or spent; it is rather a measure of saving and consumption together. To maintain that savings are not income is not illogical, however, if one is willing to go the whole way and define income as a concept already nicely covered by the word "consumption." If savings are not income, then depreciation is, not negative income; and all gain connotations must be abandoned. This, Fisher is willing to do.

The problem here is only that of choice among verbal symbols. However, it seems a hardly debatable proposition that usage is already too firmly established to permit our accepting Fisher's proposal and eschewing the gain implications of income,[82] even were there something to be gained thereby. His proposal comes all too tardily in the history of our language; and his pleas have been, and must be, without effect upon our courts, legislatures, accountants,[83] and men of affairs—not to mention the economists.

[82] This rather commonplace view is nicely expressed in C. Colin, *La Notion du revenu* (Paris, 1924): "En somme, si nous pouvons trouver chez Irving Fisher certains points de détails propres à nous aide dans nos recherches, il nous est impossible de lui demander un corps de doctrine auquel on puisse se référer absolument. Il a élaboré une idée qui lui est propre du capital et du revenu, sa conception, logique du reste avec elle-même, a cependant le grave défaut de ne s'accorder ni avec les idées économique ni avec les idées courantes, elle reste donc, en quelque sorte, 'en dehors,' et à quelque point de vue que l'on se place dans cette étude ne peut nous apporter que confusion" (p. 19).

[83] Professor Canning has said a great many nice things about Fisher's work; and he believes, or at least asserts, that it is of immense potential importance for accounting. He points out that *if* an accountant *were* measuring consumption he would come out as does Fisher; he asserts that assets have never previously been adequately defined; and he observes that accountants and directors should give thought to the consumption requirements of stock-

The case against Fisher on these grounds we take to be either altogether clear or not amenable to fruitful argument. Yet one may suggest further that to conceive income in terms of things—as consumption goods and services—is to falsify the whole valuation process. The yield of an instrument can properly be conceived only in terms of the value of the physical product which differential calculation imputes to it. That physical product may be anything upon which the market sets a price; i.e., consumption goods, consumers' capital, or intermediate goods. The value of an instrument may derive merely from its uses in making other instruments. Interest theory is only superimposed on price theory to emphasize certain important relations and certain problems of social economy. The apportionment of resources among industries producing different consumption goods presents a problem for which (hypothetical) demand schedules are ultimate data. But the demand schedules for instruments can be rationalized or explained to advantage, on the assumption that investors are seeking to maximize the rate of return upon their commitments. This rate of return or productivity of capital, unlike utility, is a useful, descriptive conception.

Before concluding this discussion, it may be well to refer briefly to the familiar question: When does income accrue? One reason the question presents difficulties is that it has been badly phrased. The notion of

---

holders in deciding upon dividend policy. These not very illuminating points aside, I fail to see that Canning has even made any contact between accounting problems and Professor Fisher's work; but both the author and Fisher seem to feel otherwise on that score. Incidentally, considerable space is given to problems of depreciation measurement! (Canning, *op. cit.*)

accrual is best reserved for assets and liabilities. Interest accrues really not as revenue or expense but as an asset or liability. The question is better stated simply as a problem in valuation: When should value changes be recognized? We do best, in general, to regard income not as something accruing or flowing with time—for such language is dangerously figurative—but merely as a result imputed to particular periods. Strictly speaking, the calculation of income demands complete revaluation of all assets and obligations at the end of every period. Practically, the question is: How shall the requisite value estimates be obtained? This is where the realization criterion may properly be introduced as a practical expedient. But the problem here is one of administration, not of definition.

We turn now to problems of defining income for purposes of taxation—confessing thus tardily that our remarks about the definition of income have been colored not a little by considerations of tax policy.

ADDENDUM

One well-known treatise, Robert Meyer's *Das Wesen des Einkommens* (Berlin, 1887), has been left for discussion in a separate note. This arrangement is dictated, first, by the fact that Meyer's treatise is a strangely confusing mixture of clear insight and dialectical puzzles and, second, because he is not representative of any very clear-cut position different from those already discussed.

Meyer's book reminds one of Neumann in its general argument and also because the author's incisive criticism of other writers is so devastating against his own position. Meyer condemns the Smithian concept, insists that Hermann only aggravated its erroneous emphasis, and condemns Mangoldt, Held,

Guth, Wagner, Malthus, and others for the same heresy. He commends Schmoller's insight (especially his criticism of Smith and his emphasis upon *Konsumtion* and *Bedarf*); and he is willing to overlook Schmoller's (unwittingly) coming-out with much the same concept in the end.

Meyer refers approvingly to Rodbertus and quotes him at length. In one passage, Rodbertus, after stating what is also Meyer's contention, that *Einkommen* is not *Produkt*, says (Meyer, *op. cit.*, p. 21): "Dagegen das Einkommen nur die Masse unmittelbaren Güter die auf der letzten Productionstufe fertig geworden sind." Wereupon Meyer criticizes him for imposing no *Maximal-Grenze*. Later Rodbertus is quoted as follows: "Er [the individual] muss also in derselben Zeit auch das Kapital un-verringert erhalten. Dadurch erhält das Einkommen seinem Umfange nach eine wirtschaftliche Beschränkung, während es seiner Natur nach stets nur unmittelbare Güter umfassen kann." This is the usual, and always unsatisfactory, method of ad-mitting the *Maximal-Grenze* quietly by the back door. But Meyer's is another attack. He says that the last clause is "un-logisch, er sollte wohl heissen 'während es seiner Natur nach alle unmittelbare Güter umfasst.'" Having thus repaired the mas-ter's language, Meyer proceeds to reject the position, saying: "Die R. 'sche Definition setzt uns in völligen Widerspruch mit dem ausnahmslos herrschenden Sprachgebrauch, der das Ein-kommen von der wirklichen Verzehrung deutlich unterscheidet."

Waiving the question of whether this remark is apposite, and reading on, one finds Meyer flirting with the *Regelmässigkeit* criterion. But he soon disavows serious intentions in this affair; indeed, he criticizes this criterion quite judiciously, in a manner suggestive of Neumann and even of Popitz' pointed comments. The true definition which finally emerges, however, really differs from Neumann's only in being less frankly evasive. In the fol-lowing passage, which is the denouement of the mystery, *Regel-mässigkeit* is back again and, if I can read German, without any evidence of its chastisement:

Soll daher die Beziehung zur Konsumtion, die Konsumtabilität als charakterisches Merkmal des Einkommens festgehalten werden, wozu der wissenschaftliche wie der vulgäre Sprachgebrauch unabweislich nötigen, so darf diese Beziehung nicht durch die Substitution des Merkmals der Wiederkehr hergestellt werden, sie muss als selbständiges Merkmal des Einkommens verlangt werden. . . . . Soll nun dem Einkommen auch die Eigenschaft der Wiederkehr zukommen, so müssen wir sie als vollkommen selbständiges Merkmal dem ersten an der Seite stellen. Zugleich werden wir aber das Ergebnis der oben angestellten Untersuchung, dass wir es in der Wiederkehr nicht mit einer irgend welchen Einnahmen anhaftenden Eigerschaft, sondern mit einem Erfolg zu tun haben, der unserer Wirtschaftführung erst vorschwebt, der künftige Arbeitsaufwendung und gewisse gegenwärtige wirtschaftliche Vorkehrungen bedingt ist, entsprechend Rechnung tragen müssen. Diesen Gesichtspunkten entsprechend, müsste unter Einkommen eine, in einer bestimmten Periode eingehende Menge von Genussgütern (Güter erster Ordnung), deren nach Massgabe des Bedarfs wiederkehrende Herbeischaffung gesichert ist, verstanden werden [p. 78].

Incidentally, Meyer (toward the end of chap. iv, in which the foregoing passage appears) dismisses, in the best German manner, the question of how *Einkommen* could be measured. The question is recognized as difficult, is left unilluminated; and the discussion proceeds in terms of the greater ultimate importance of clarity in the abstract idea.

CHAPTER IV

PREFACING DISCUSSION OF
SPECIAL PROBLEMS

REQUIREMENTS of rigorous definition and considerations of equity in taxation may well lead to similar description of income. The concepts of economics are, in a pragmatic sense, merely tools for analyzing specific problems of public policy and social control; and there is surely some presumption that concepts useful for analyzing results of policies will also have important place in satisfactory schemes of positive control. That graduated taxation on the basis of what we have defined as income represents the best means of avoiding or minimizing arbitrary discrimination is not amenable to simple demonstration. Such a conclusion may be drawn appropriately only from the consideration of special problems of income taxation.

If one accepts our definition of income, one may be surprised that it has ever been proposed seriously as a basis for taxation. Income, so conceived, would be readily and accurately measurable only in a world where goods and services fell neatly into a small number of homogeneous classes; also, where definite market prices were available at all times for evaluation of all commodities and capital assets in existence. This implies perhaps, among other things, costless transportation and indestructible factors! In fact, incomes represent at best only estimates of a very tentative sort. The calculation is simple only where persons own no property except of a kind which has definite, ascertainable market prices, i.e., where property exists only in the form of securities actively traded on the exchanges.

How, then, can income be employed as a tax base? The undertaking might well seem to involve insuperable difficulties. But income taxes are numerous today;[1] and, in England and Germany, they have a long and instructive history. The practical problems for such taxation are best to be understood in terms of experience in these and other countries.

One may remark at the outset that no government has ever undertaken to graduate taxes really on the basis of personal income.[2] The actual tax base is merely something calculated according to more or less carefully defined methods; and these methods may be regarded as designed to give results which are in most instances something like true personal income.[3] Indeed, every income tax is, and probably must be, based largely on

[1] According to J. Popitz ("Einkommensteuer," in *Handw. der Staatswissenschaft* [4th ed.], III, 439), in 1926 there were 124 income-tax laws in force in various parts of the world. There are many more now.

[2] This point is nicely expressed by G. Colm, in a manner suggestive of Popitz' comment on *Quellentheorie* (see above, chap. iii, p. 78, n. 49): "Wir suchen Einkommen grundsätzlich als Einkommen der Verbrauchswirtschaft aufzufassen, während diese steuerliche Begriffsfassung gerade umgekehrt vom Einkommen als Einkommen einer Erwerbswirtschaft ausgeht und diese Vorstellung dann auf die Verbrauchswirtschaft überträgt." "Grundsätzliche Bemerkungen zum Begriff des Volkseinkommen und des Volksvermögens," (*Schriften des Vereins für Sozialpolitik*, CLXXIII, 30).

[3] The English income tax involves perhaps the farthest departure from the essentially personal connotations of income. Of it, Popitz says: "Diese Zerlegung [into the Schedules] ist so stark durchgeführt, dass man der Income Tax überhaupt den Charakter einer Einkommensteuer abgesprochen und von einem Bündel von Ertragssteuern ohne inneren Zusammenhang gesprochen

presumptions.[4] With respect to business enterprises, tax laws and administrative regulations usually take over conventional accounting rules.[5] More generally, the government assumes the task of preventing concealment or omission of positive items and places upon the taxpayers the burden of proof as to the proper deductions. Tax laws do not really define income but merely set up rules as to what must be included and what may be deducted; and such rules by no means define income because they are neither exhaustive nor logically coherent. That rules of this kind work out at all well is due to the co-operation of taxpayers, the paucity of ingenious lies, and to the availability of checks, in market prices, in information derived from third parties, and in the mass of business records and accounts.

Since the devices of accounting and tax legislation contemplate only very rough approximation to income, it is decisively important to see behind these methods

---

hat (so der österreichische Verwaltungsgerichtshof)" (*op. cit.*, p. 467). Teschemacher, in *Handbuch der Finanzwissenschaft* (Tübingen, 1926), II, 110, quotes with approval Vocke's familiar characterization of the English tax as an "Ertragssteuer mit Einkommensteuermomenten."

[4] We use "presumptions" rather broadly here. It would be interesting to list various kinds of presumptions, starting with the simpler provisions of Schedule B in England and the more complicated provisions of the Impôt Cédulaire in France and proceeding to (or through) the taxation of dividends under the American law. The foregoing quotation from Colm suggests rather nicely the broader implications of the presumption idea (p. 104, n. 2).

[5] In Germany accounting practices have long been regulated by law. Many taxpayers are required to keep their accounts according to the provisions of the *Handelsgesetzbuch;* and the system prescribed is naturally adopted more widely (see Hatfield, *Modern Accounting* [1909], *passim*).

Our own federal tax stumbled rather tardily into reasonable conformity with accounting practice (Act of September, 1916). The accrual procedures, however, received extralegal, administrative sanction still earlier.

of calculation an "ideal income," calculable by different and less practicable methods. Only on the basis of some broader conception is it possible to criticize and evaluate merely practicable procedures and to consider fruitfully the problem of bettering the system of presumptions. Indeed, if there be any excuse for a treatise like this, it must lie in the importance of maintaining some broad —and perhaps quite "impractical"—conception in terms of which existing and proposed practices in income taxation may be examined, tested, and criticized.[6]

In the chapters following we shall be concerned with problems of income taxation from the point of view of discrimination. Reference to our general definition may be somewhat infrequent; but the reader is urged to consider how consistently the obvious considerations of justice lead to conclusions implicit in the definition. Indeed, it may be regarded as a sort of thesis that income, as already described, is essentially identical with that base on which it would be most nearly equitable to levy upon individuals. At all events, we shall henceforth be concerned largely with implications of the proposition that taxes should bear similarly upon persons similarly situated.

To have a proper basis for testing the definition in terms of discrimination, one must recognize the inescapable limitations inherent in even the ideal income tax. The necessity of arbitrary delimination of "income in kind" and of inadequate distinction between consump-

---

[6] And we would maintain emphatically that no ideas of utility, or of recurrence, regularity, separation, realization, and their variants, have any place in this ultimate, ideal conception. Most of them lack even the small merit of suggesting simplifications for practice.

tion and business expense make some inequities unavoidable. Changes in price levels will likewise lead to some injustice under any conceivable tax system. Nor is it possible to devise adequate differentiation between incomes earned and unearned, precarious and certain, stable and fluctuating. Moreover, the family, not the individual, is the prevailing economic unit; and it is obviously impossible to differentiate perfectly according to the size and age composition of such groups. Incidentally, taxation of income, to many, will seem to favor unduly the person who "consumes" inherited capital as well as the income therefrom.[7] These, and other, limitations are simply inherent in income taxation per se. To them must be added those which arise in the actual measurement of incomes, according to imperfect legislative rules and under imperfect administration.

A deal of inequity must arise from the inadequacies of legal presumptions and from arbitrary administrative regulations. Here and there individuals will find established procedure working, now to their advantage, and now against them. Such casual, fortuitous discrimination, however, represents only the inevitable consequence of compromise between ideal and feasible methods and need not seriously impair the operation of the tax instrument.[8] So, in the study of policy, it is proper

[7] Everyone should be permitted some inconsistency. We freely confess our approval of the practice of treating consumption as a lower limit in the calculation of taxable income—a practice followed partially in the German tax (*Reichseinkommensteuer* [1925], sec. 49). This view may find approval among those who are able to argue that ordinary income taxes discriminate against saving.

[8] Though, of course, such discrimination may be important for one concerned with the choice between this and other tax devices.

to focus attention especially upon those shortcomings of tax methods which give rise to opportunities for systematic evasion.[9] The taxpayer will frequently be able, without impairing his income much, if at all, to order his affairs in such manner as to take advantage of imperfections in the tax system. Where such opportunities are numerous and are open to many taxpayers, fiscal machinery is seriously defective. Nor are the unfortunate consequences merely those of the moment. As evasive practices become more and more widespread and reach the attention of the community at large, the task of administration becomes increasingly difficult, merely because of change in the attitudes of persons as taxpayers (and as administrators). Income taxes per se are perhaps even more difficult to administer than are taxes on general property. At present one works fairly well, and the other fails miserably. Surely one may hope that time will not bring both these fiscal instruments to the same fate. Yet this is to be avoided only if the naïve faith of taxpayers in the fairness of the law and effectiveness of its administration can be preserved—which is to say, only if a substantial similarity of taxation can be maintained among persons of substantially similar circumstances.[10]

Administrators may not concern themselves greatly

[9] Or "avoidance," if one does really prefer that term for "legal evasion."

[10] Income taxes do have a great advantage over property taxes, of course, as regards taxpayer co-operation and resistance, in that the former employs an obviously more equitable base; also, in that the payments do not continue evenly and relentlessly during periods of business misfortune and financial loss. Moreover, they permit of offsets and internal checks not available under the property-tax form. Still, it must be regarded as perfectly possible that income taxes should go the way of the personal-property tax.

about considerations of justice; but they should be vitally concerned as to whether levies like the income tax are generally felt to be clearly inequitable. This feeling, we venture, is more likely to arise where persons are seen to pay very different taxes for no good reason, or to pay similarly when difference is clearly appropriate, than where the general level of rates or degree of progression is high for all alike. Thus, avoidance of obvious and flagrant inequity is imperative if income taxes are to be cheaply and effectively administered. If they are to afford important means of social control, the requirements are still more severe.

We turn now to various problems involved in making income taxation more equitable.

CHAPTER V

INCOME IN KIND

MEASUREMENT of consumption presents insuperable difficulties to achievement of a rigorous conception of personal income. The conundrums propounded by Kleinwächter cannot be solved satisfactorily by any definite sort of rule or formula. Likewise, from the point of view of equity in taxation, the consumption of goods and services produced within the household or individual economy presents real imponderables. Clearly inequitable results arise whether such items are consistently included or ignored.

To exclude them is obviously to penalize specialization. If A works nine hours a day and pays for care of his garden with the proceeds of one hour's work, he would be overtaxed relative to B, who works eight hours at the same hourly rate and maintains a similar garden by giving daily one hour of his own time. Families where wives pay for their housework from their own earnings outside the home would also be relatively overtaxed. Similar cases might be multiplied *ad nauseam*.

On the other hand, if the value of goods and services produced within the household are to be accounted for, one must face, first of all, the necessity of stopping somewhere; and no convenient stopping-place is discernible. Shall one include the value of shaves? of instruction to children? of a mother's services as a nurse?

But further problems appear. Even if one be satisfied with the decision to include only the sort of goods and services commonly obtained by exchange (and such a rule is certainly not very helpful), the results will often seem unfair. Mrs. A does her own housework, while Mrs. B prefers to economize on other things and hires a maid. To impose additional taxes upon the A family is, so to speak, to penalize industry and subsidize leisure —and in a not readily defensible manner. If Mrs. A prefers to do her own work and spend on good entertainment what would otherwise go as wages to a maid rather than have time for bridge and modern fiction, it is hard to see why more income tax should be imposed on that account. The enjoyment of leisure is merely a form of consumption; and the choice between leisure and goods is of the same order as that among economic goods generally. Surely there is a strong presumption against any differentiation, under income taxes, according to the form which one's consumption may take.[1]

All this, however, may only suggest the impropriety of taxing as income what may be called "earned income in kind." If it is not equitable to exclude such items entirely, this may be recognized in the most flagrant cases by allowing small, additional exemption with respect to the "earned income" of a wife—as is done under the English income tax.[2] In general, however, it would

---

[1] It may seem strange that we should invoke this view of "leisure as income" merely in this relatively unimportant connection. Apology lies perhaps in the importance of its implications here in principle. Of course, it may contribute handsomely to the case for differentiation and for supplementary levies upon "pure property incomes."

[2] Sec. 18, Act of 1920, provided for exemption of nine-tenths of the wife's

seem that considerations of justice, not to mention those of administration, argue here for rather narrow definition of taxable income.

On the other hand, when property is employed directly in consumption uses, there is the strongest case for recognizing an addition to taxable income. This is widely recognized in criticism of our federal tax for its egregious discrimination between renters and homeowners, and perhaps more strikingly in the almost consistently different practice among income taxes abroad.[3]

---

earned income up to an amount not exceeding £45. In the case of a wife earning, say, £52, this allowance, together with the allowance of one-sixth with respect to total earned income, made possible reduction of family taxable income on account of the wife's earnings by an amount greater than her earnings. This anomaly is removed by amendment of 1928, whereby allowance is reduced to five-sixths of the wife's earnings but not exceeding £45. See V. Walton, *Income Tax* (London, 1928), pp. 116–17.

[3] Rental income to homeowners is reached in the English tax under Schedule A. The basis is annual value or rack rent, with a repair deduction varying from one-fourth on small properties to slightly more than one-sixth for properties of high annual value. See Newport, *Income Tax Law and Practice* (London, 1927), p. 43. For the German practice see *Reichseinkommensteuergesetz* (1925), sec. 14.

Popitz remarks that the tax laws in most countries count rental income to homeowners as taxable income and then observes: "In den aussereuropäischen Staaten mit anderen Wohnungsüblichkeiten gehört vielfach die Nutzung der eigenen Wohnung nicht zum Einkommen (so z. B. in den australischen Staaten)" (*Handwörterbuch der Staatswissenschaft* [4th ed.], III, 407–8). The difference in *Wohnungsüblichkeiten* may help to explain this fact; but surely it is a meager sort of apology. At all events, the United States and Canada seem to be the only important countries not taxing rental income to homeowners. For practice in the Australian Commonwealth tax see below, p. 117.

Schanz (writing in 1896!) remarks that he knows of only one jurisdiction where rental income to homeowners is excluded. This is in Mecklenburg. He points out that a similar situation existed in Basel from 1840 to 1866. He also mentions the United States tax of 1894 but finds the text of the law ambiguous on the point in question (*Finanz Archiv*, 1896, p. 35).

On what grounds may one defend this policy of including one sort of income in kind and ignoring the other? The answer, in general terms, is that the exemption of *"earned* income in kind" leads to no serious inequity in the distribution of the tax burden. Such income bulks large only in the case of classes exempt from tax or subject to only the lowest rates. Moreover, this element of income probably shows rather little variation within income classes and diminishes in a fairly continuous manner as one ascends the income scale. Certainly, it will seldom represent a significant percentage of total income in the case of persons subject to the higher rates of tax. There is, furthermore, the compensating effect of the fact that "leisure income" is not included within the tax base. Thus, to ignore "earned income in kind" serves, on the whole, merely to increase both the real exemptions and the real degree of progression; i.e., it leads to a true progression somewhat steeper than that revealed in the nominal rates.

It is perhaps equally significant that this sort of exclusion or exemption gives rise to only a fortuitous sort of discrimination and does not really facilitate evasion. The opportunities for tax avoidance by changing the form of one's receipts are meager indeed, the premium on specialization being far too great. One cannot go far toward making one's family an autonomous economy without severe penalty!

If such considerations support exemption of the one class of items, they argue quite as strongly for inclusion of the other. Income from consumers' capital is often a large part of total income for individuals in the upper brackets. To exclude it is to introduce a bias inconsistent with the system of progression and to differentiate flagrantly among persons of really similar financial circumstances. Furthermore, where such income is excluded, an attractive and easy means of evasion is made available. The use of property rights to obtain purchasing power is penalized as against more direct employment. Investments in industry may be liquidated, and the proceeds used to obtain property for consumption use.

Serious inequity arises, furthermore, from the fact that the opportunity for evasion is open to different income classes, and to members within given classes, on very different terms. If consumers' capital provided a relatively uniform percentage of true income among persons of the same income class, and if the amount or percentage of such property income increased in fairly continuous manner from one income class to the next above, then adjustment for the exemption might be worked out merely in the scale of rates. But even the first of these conditions is certainly not fulfilled; nor can continued exploitation of the opportunities for tax avoidance be expected to bring it about. The direct employment of capital is far from equally feasible for different kinds of consumption or for different people with similar consumption tastes. He who chooses to travel, to spend time at watering places, on hunting trips, or archeological expeditions, suffers by comparison with his friends who are content to enjoy the luxury of a half-dozen owned residences, with their art galleries, golf courses, beaches, etc.[4] Among the upper middle class, the tax will penalize severely those whose occupation makes homeowning undesirable. It will penalize those actually engaged in business and favor those who merely clip coupons. It will discriminate especially against persons of large unfunded income and, one may add, against people living in communities afflicted with zealous realtors where one must lay heavy bets on the future in order to become a homeowner.[5] The real opportunity to escape tax thus varies widely, according to the consumption tastes of individuals, according to the amount of property held, and according to the character of one's occupation and investments. Surely the United States and Canada have much to learn from the rest of the world with respect to this phase of income taxation.

It has been suggested, as a simple remedy, that taxpayers be allowed to make deduction of rent paid for residences.[6] If no more thoroughgoing reform is obtain-

[4] Though the government, to be sure, will subsidize travel in one's own yacht or motorcar!

[5] One may mention too the severe discrimination as between the rural and urban population.

[6] This was permitted under our Civil War income taxes, the provision being first introduced in the Act of March 3, 1863 (sec. 11). Professor F. Flügel (*The Income Tax as Applied to Individuals* [Berlin, 1927]) has evidently read carelessly in sec. 117, Act of March 3, 1865, for he says (p. 14, n. 4): "In 1865 house owners in turn were granted the privilege of deducting the rental value of their premises." The language of the act is not happy; but certainly it does not say that owners may deduct rental values; rather, that rents paid shall be deductible and rental values to owners not included. One might easily interpret the language as Flügel has if one neglected to read the full statement in the law.

F. J. Neumann (*Grundlagen der Volkswirtschaftslehre* [Tübingen, 1899])

able, the plan deserves support. But its shortcomings are by no means slight. It would be tantamount to subsidy for one type of consumption and would thus discriminate unreasonably among persons of different habits and tastes. Moreover, it would favor unduly those whose rental contracts called for special services not ordinarily provided by landlords—residents in hotels and furnished apartments, especially—or would require separate valuation and deduction of such services. The deduction of rent in full, moreover, would simply reverse the discrimination, since the homeowner, under a more adequate system, would surely be entitled to deduction for depreciation; and, if the law were so generous to renters, homeowners might well claim that they should be allowed to deduct repair and maintenance costs ordinarily borne by landlords. Legislation and administration might take account of all these considerations; but the plan would thereby be deprived of its great merit of simplicity. At worst, however, it would be an improvement over our present system.

The English practice of assessing the occupier[7] upon the rental value of real property, less an arbitrary de-

maintains (p. 228) that many tax laws have adopted the expedient of permitting deduction for renters. However, he cites only the income-tax law of Basel in 1866; and he remarks (p. 228, n. 226) that the practice was later abandoned there (see also p. 93, n. 70). The change in Basel was made in 1880 and the now prevailing Continental practice adopted. See Schanz, *Finanz Archiv*, 1896, p. 35; and, for detail, see his *Steuern der Schweiz*, II, 34–56.

[7] For supertax (or, as the law says now, surtax), the assessment is upon the owner, of course, but the amount is determined by the income-tax assessment.

preciation allowance,[8] could not easily be followed in America. It depends, first of all, upon a general system of collection at source—a system involving considerable departure from true personal income taxation in the direction of mere *Ertragssteuern*. Difficulties arise also from our relative unfamiliarity with annual values. An alternative procedure, however, of the kind followed in the Australian Commonwealth, appears to be especially promising.

Under the Australian law, there is assessed as taxable income "5 per cent of the capital value of land with improvements thereon owned and used or used rent free by the taxpayer for residence or enjoyment and not for profit."[9] A conspicuous advantage of this method lies in the avoidance of the depreciation problem—which, by the way, is very inadequately handled under rules of the kind prescribed in Schedule A of the English law. If a rate representing a conservative interest return is applied to capital value, one should get directly something which approximates net annual value or net return from ownership. To be sure, the property must be valued; but assessments must be made in any event for purposes of other levies. If this work is now badly done under the property taxes, we need not be reconciled to indefinite continuance of present conditions of administration; and the general program of co-operation between the tax-administering agencies of the federal, state, and local governments has much to commend it.

[8] For details regarding these allowances see above, p. 112, n. 3; also, Newport, *op. cit.*, p. 42.

[9] *Income Taxes in the British Dominions* (London, 1923), p. 238.

If federal officials had need of good assessments on residence properties, income-tax collection might become more costly for a time. But their activities might contribute greatly toward improvement of state and local administration. Even if the administration of such a provision did cost the federal government more than the additional revenue resulting from the broadening of the tax base, the plan might still be defended, for reasons already suggested, or merely for its effect upon the equitableness of the income tax as a whole. If revenue agents relied merely upon existing local assessments, with perhaps occasional investigation, the income tax would be distinctly more equitable in its relative burdens than with complete exemption of such income in kind.

To recognize the importance of including this item in the tax base is to raise question as to where one may stop. If it be so important to include return from real property used within the owner's household, is it not also desirable to proceed similarly with regard to furniture, fixtures, automobiles, art collections, yachts, and other personal property, especially that devoted to luxury or invidious consumption?[10]

It is advantageous to recognize, first of all, that the error involved in ignoring consumption income from property varies directly with the durability or service

[10] Robert Meyer (*Das Wesen des Einkommens* [Berlin, 1887], chap. vii) is the only important writer who rejects in principle the treatment of *Güternutzungen* as income. His position seems to follow from the least intelligible of his ideas about *Einkommenbegriff* (*Einkommen* as *eine Menge von Genussgütern*). Schanz's criticism (*Finanz Archiv*, 1896, p. 17) is brief, pointed, and adequate.

life of the kind of property in question. In the case of clothing, the difference between the value of its use and its original cost is obviously small; with most foods, to take an extreme case, the difference is simply negligible. In general, the disregard of income in kind from the less durable forms of personal tangibles will occasion no serious inequities in relative tax burdens.

At risk of serious digression, let us consider here a problem which has not yet received proper attention. Consumption, presumably, should be measured in terms of values at the time of consumption; but to ignore changes in value between time of purchase and time of use will ordinarily make very little difference. The difference might be large, of course, where a man purchased choice beverages and allowed them to acquire the quality and distinction of ripe age—especially if prohibition came in the interim. At all events, there is suggested here the difficult question of where to draw the line between acquisition of means and their employment. At what point shall the idea of gain and loss be dropped? One finds no ready answer; but the necessity of drawing some line is clear.

If one is to define consumption as something measurable—as something more nearly quantitative, conceptually, than ultimate psychic benefits—one must include outlays for many things which only stupidity, ignorance, and gullibility would ever lead consumers to purchase. To abandon amounts paid and market prices as measures is to leave one's self stranded in the intellectual desert of subjective values and psychic *numéraires*. An ideal income tax would perhaps differentiate among individuals according to their talents for using funds in consumption; but, until some adequate, objective index of such abilities is forthcoming, income taxes must worry along with measurable quantities!

Professor Canning maintains[11] that, if one purchases a vacuum cleaner and finds that it will not sweep, this fact must be recognized in the computation of "final income." Such a proposition may seem too obvious to question; yet one may apply the same line of argument to purchases of patent cures that cure nothing, informational literature that misinforms, and almost everything sold by false representations. In general, there is presumption against admitting exceptions to the rule that consumption, as an element of income, must be measured, in the case of things obtained by exchange, by outlays for consumption purposes. Even Canning's vacuum cleaner can hardly escape this presumption. (Here ends the digression.)

No doubt there are possibilities in the use of presumptions with respect to income in kind from personal property. Roscher contends that expenditure for clothing and household effects displays rather uniform relation to other consumption income and might thus be neglected for tax purposes.[12] If such proportionality were realized approximately and with rare exceptions,

[11] *Economics and Accountancy* (New York, 1929), p. 166.

[12] "Für Steuerzwecke, wo es mehr auf verhältnismässige als auf absolute Schätzung ankommt, würde die Annahme hinreichen, dass jede Privatwirtschaft nach Massgabe ihres übrigen Einkommens Gerät und Kleider gebrauche. Man könnte diesen Posten also unbedenklich weglassen" (Roscher, *Grundlagen der N. Ö.*, § 146 [quoted in Schanz, *Finanz Archiv*, 1896, p. 38, n. 2]).

With progressive taxation, the case for ignoring such items obviously disappears. Schanz denies the propriety of Roscher's presumption. B. Moll ad-

or if any simple relation between income in kind from personal property and other income might reasonably be assumed, then allowance for exclusion of such items might be made merely by appropriate adjustment of the scale of tax rates.

Such a plan has at least two shortcomings. First, no presumption based on total income could fail to work very badly in individual cases. Besides, even if this were not true, it is rather absurd to suspect that inclusion or exclusion of such income in kind would really cause legislatures to maintain a rate system appropriately different on that account from what it would otherwise have been.

A better plan surely would be that of using some multiple of home rentals (and, if the Australian methods were employed, a different multiple of net rental income), on the presumably reasonable grounds that net rental values of furniture will correlate highly with the annual value of real property used for residence. A certain percentage of residence rent or value might simply be added to the tax base as computed without regard to these provisions. The actual percentages—and they probably should vary with the residence rent or value—might be determined from statistical studies. Some such arrangement does seem commendable, being simple in application and requiring no additional information except from renters.

Neglect of these factors in true personal income is

---

vances argument against Roscher in which I am unable to find either meaning or relevance, though I concur heartily with almost everything Moll says about problems of income definition and income taxation (see Moll, *Probleme der Finanzwissenschaft* [Leipzig, 1924], p. 152).

clearly unfortunate. However, the only practicable alternative is the employment of fairly simple presumptions.[13] The measures we have suggested might well be supplemented by special provisions with respect to such things as yachts, art collections, automobiles, and other more durable articles. Here, too, the appropriate additions to taxable income might be determined on the basis of capital values.

Receipts in kind may also take the form of compensation for services rendered. Our federal law provides for inclusion of compensation of whatever kind and in whatever form paid.[14] However, the value of perquisites, like board and living quarters, is not taxable if these facilities are provided by the employer for his own convenience. The courts and the treasury distinguish strangely between cases where the taxpayer effects a saving but receives no income and those where the perquisites may be regarded as additional compensation.[15] In England perquisites are taxable as income only in cases where the taxpayer is free to convert them into cash.[16]

---

[13] Schanz (*Finanz Archiv*, 1896, p. 39) proposes addition to other income of 3 per cent of the amount for which household effects are insured against fire. Insurance practices being so divergent, this looks merely like another tax upon insurance, not like a part of an income tax!

[14] Revenue Act of 1928, sec. 22a.

[15] *Regulations 74*, Art. 53 (Montgomery, *Income Tax Procedure* [New York, 1926]). Exemption is granted by Congress with respect to the rental value of dwelling-house and appurtenances thereto furnished to a minister of the gospel! (sec. 22b, 8). Furthermore, "the value of quarters furnished Army and Navy officers, members of the Coast Guard, Coast and Geodic Survey, and Public Health Service, or amounts received as commutation of quarters by such officers or members, do not constitute taxable income" (*Regulations 74*, Art. 53).

[16] This rule seems to involve an interesting variant of the realization cri-

Such arbitrary rules do invite caustic criticism. Anyone who condemns them hastily, however, will be placed in a most awkward position by a request for constructive proposals. There is here an essential and insuperable difficulty, even in principle. The problem of Kleinwächter's *Flügeladjutant* is insoluble and certainly is not amenable to reasonable solution on the basis of simple rules which could be administered by revenue agents. Obviously there are many instances where taxpayers are too favorably treated. The sporting-goods salesman, who lives at the best hotels and clubs and spends much time entertaining good customers "on the company," might well be taxed on something more than his salary —providing he doesn't dislike such life, as the *Flügeladjutant* did the operas! Yet, after all, these are merely one kind of perquisite. Other positions may be equally attractive, at the same nominal salary, for prestige, freedom, leisure, or what not. And one must surely hesitate to propose graduation under income taxes according to the pleasurableness of people's occupations.

The taxation of compensation in kind, under our own law, presents another instance of clear discrimination against recipients of personal-service incomes. If one obtains use of one's residence as part of one's salary, the rental value must be included for income tax. On the

---

terion. In *Tennant* v. *Smith* (1892 A.C. 150) the lord chancellor said: "This is an Income Tax Act, and what is intended to be taxed is income. . . . . I am of the opinion, in the words of Lord Young, that the thing sought to be taxed is not income unless it can be turned into money." See also *Corke* v. *Fry* (C.S. 1895), where rental value of manse was held taxable as income because minister had power to let the property (cases cited in Murray and Carter, *Guide to Income Tax Practice* [11th ed.], pp. 304 and 395).

other hand, a neighbor, obtaining use of an identical house by virtue of ownership in fee, is quite exempt so far as concerns this item. Indeed, he may even deduct a part of the rental value, in effect, if the property has been purchased or retained through borrowing.

Compensation in kind will ordinarily be small and confined largely to people at the bottom of the income scale. The rules now followed by our treasury insure against serious evasion and permit of equitable adjustment in the rare cases where perquisites may be a large item in large incomes. At all events, let it be recognized that one faces here one of the real imponderables of income definition.

CHAPTER VI

GRATUITOUS RECEIPTS

THE ordinary notion of income is one which excludes items like inheritances and bequests. With respect to gifts, the nature of popular usage is less clear. The definition of income which we have proposed, on the other hand, would bring all these items of receipts into the calculation. To exclude them would require introducing into the definition a distinction between one-sided transfers and payments in the nature of fair compensation. If one seeks simplicity and elegance, such distinctions, rested as they must be on questions of motive, are certainly to be avoided so far as possible.

The conception of personal income as the algebraic sum of the individual's consumption and the change in the value of his property rights during a period is, we believe, less ambiguous, more definite, and more readily intelligible than any alternative conception which merits consideration as a basis for personal taxation. It is our contention, moreover, that the conception which admits of most elegant definition is also the one which affords the basis for most nearly equitable taxation and for legislation which minimizes the difficulties of interpretation and administration and the possibilities of systematic avoidance. Some students may accept this view as immediately obvious or axiomatic. But it is unnecessary and undesirable to rest one's case on such broad grounds.

It remains, therefore, to consider how the particular arrangements might be worked out and to touch upon some relevant questions as to the definition of consumption.

There is now little dispute as to the propriety of taxing gifts, inheritances, and bequests. The phenomenal development of death duties during the last half-century reflects a nearly unanimous indorsement of substantial limitation upon the right of inheritance, and of taxes upon one-sided transfers as the proper means to that end. One finds here a tragic discrepancy, to be sure, between aspirations and achievements. A great movement has been dissipated in small and illusory successes; and much fine zeal has been squandered on those ill-conceived expedients which legislation now contains. The end here has been espoused and pursued with a haste and enthusiasm which have not paused for definition of the end or for careful study of the appropriate means. Thus, while there is no issue as to whether gratuitous transfers should be taxed, the question of methods remains. Whether they should be treated as taxable personal income, moreover, can usefully be discussed only as part of the larger question as to the appropriate form (or forms) of levy with respect to such transfers.

Though conceding that income is best defined broadly to include gifts, inheritances, and bequests, one might argue for the exemption of such items under a progressive personal tax. Several prominent writers have taken this position, on the grounds that the receipts in question are already subject to special levies.[1] This is one

[1] Such naïve notions regarding "offsets" are commonplace in the literature of taxation. It is interesting here only to note instances of the heresy in

of the most spurious and naïve types of argument in the literature—and one which is encountered repeatedly. It is especially interesting here, since it involves an unwitting reversion to *Quellentheorie* on the part of writers who have condemned such doctrines most emphatically.[2]

That the reasonableness of particular levies should be appraised with regard for the tax system as a whole is a venerable and respected commonplace. It is always possible that the imperfections of particular taxes, as separately appraised, might be of a counteracting or offsetting nature. Such propositions, being patently too true, should always put the reader on his guard; and this one especially is notable less for its uses than for its abuses. There is no single criterion for judging the reasonableness of every particular tax or of the whole system; and actually there are many levies which must fail of justification in terms of any respectable criteria. Thus, the greatest caution is necessary in argument which appeals to offsets among different parts of the

---

the case of two writers with whom it is surprising, in the light of their other views, and inconsistent. The idea is accepted quite uncritically by Schanz (who may perhaps be pardoned, in view of the meager contemporary development of progression) and even more unreservedly by Popitz. See Schanz, "Der Einkommenbegriff und die Einkommensteuergesetze," *Finanz Archiv*, Vol. XIII (1896), pp. 72–75, esp. p. 74, where he says: "Wenn Bayern Immobiliarschenkungen mit 2% trifft, Mobiliarschenkungen dagegen nur, insoweit darüber notarielle Verträge abgeschlossen werden und auch die nur mit 3‰ und bei Verwandten nur mit 1½‰ so wird man gewiss sagen können, die Mobiliarschenkungen sind ungenügend besteuert. Es hätte da einen Sinn, in einem Einkommensteuergesetz zu sagen: Immobiliarschenkungen sind frei, Mobiliarschenkungen sind einkommensteuerpflichtig." See also J. Popitz ("Einkommensteuer," in *Handwörterbuch der Staatswissenschaft*), who also defends other exemptions (such as that of unearned increments) on the same grounds.

[2] The striking instance again is that of Popitz (*op. cit.*).

system; and nowhere is such argument more treacherous than in the case of progressive personal taxes. The fact that we have impersonal taxes on real estate is no reason for the levying of income taxes without regard for the rental income of home owners. Whether lottery prizes or "unearned increments" are taxed as such is largely irrelevant to the question of whether they should be brought into the calculation of taxable personal income. And the same must be said of gifts, inheritances, and bequests.

The income tax is not a tax upon income but a tax upon persons according to their respective incomes; and, subject to the requirement of adherence to simple, general rules, the objective of policy must be fairness among persons, not fairness among kinds of receipts (whatever that might be construed to mean). Death duties and gift taxes, in the main, are levies upon things or upon acts of transfer; they are essentially *ad rem* charges which take no account of the total circumstances of the recipient. If income, as we define it, is a proper basis for personal taxation, then the fact that certain receipts are taxed separately as such is, at most, but a crude and utterly uncompensating offset to their exclusion in the determination of taxable income; for equity in personal taxation, with exemptions and progressive rates, requires that persons of very different income circumstances should pay very different additional taxes by virtue of the same particular receipts.

Such argument nowise denies, on the other hand, that the inclusion of gratuitous receipts under the income tax might call for drastic change in our existing death duties and gift taxes. The rates under these levies, if appropriate before the receipts in question were reached as income, would certainly be inappropriate afterward; indeed, a case might be made for entire repeal of the old levies. Many writers, in discussing questions of income taxation, seem half-consciously to assume that other taxes are immutable, or to imply that income-tax reform must defer scrupulously to the squatter rights of pre-established levies. If we were under the necessity of building an income tax without alteration of existing death duties, many awkward and unhappy compromises would obviously be required. Such a conception of the problem of policy, however, deserves little place in any broad inquiry. It may be easy and convenient, in the writing of short papers and textbooks, to distinguish sharply between the problems of income and inheritance taxation; but such separation must result in an evading and obscuring of issues which intelligent inquiry should squarely face. Where adjustments should be made, in the face of an objectionable sort of multiple taxation, will properly be determined with regard for the tax system as a whole and not according to the priority of the different levies in time. If a proposed change requires accommodating adjustments in other parts of the system, judicious appraisal of the proposal will seek to determine whether all the changes involved would yield a substantial net improvement of the system.

Two questions especially may concern us here: (1) Would the inclusion of gratuitous receipts constitute a substantial improvement of the income tax, with respect to its fairness among persons, the simplicity of its under-

lying rules, and its possibilities of effective enforcement?
(2) Is there much to be lost if, to accommodate this
change, we largely abandon the established and traditional methods of taxing estates, inheritances, bequests,
and gifts?

The first question need not detain us here. That the
definition of taxable income as the algebraic sum of consumption and accumulation affords the best available
basis for personal taxation is the central thesis of our
whole discussion; and the argument must be appraised
as a whole. The inclusion of gratuitous receipts is here
proposed as part of a whole scheme of income-tax procedure—as a part consistent with, and complementary
to, the other parts, defined by the proposals of other
chapters. Thus, the proposal cannot adequately be
judged apart from other proposals which remain to be
submitted; within different general schemes of income-
tax reform, it might have no proper place at all.

Our answer to the second question has likewise been
indicated in advance. The growth of death duties is one
of the conspicuous and significant developments in modern fiscal systems. It reflects an increasing concern
about justice in taxation and a disposition among legislatures to face inequality as a real problem. These
taxes, however, are far more important for the purposes
they express than for their contribution to governmental
revenues. With large exemptions, with rates which become substantial only for fabulous transfers, with relationship discrimination, and with the inevitable shortcomings of such taxation in the hands of the separate
states, we have made only feeble gestures toward limita-

tion of inheritance. Moreover, along established lines, no effective realization of the underlying purposes seems possible at all. Existing methods of inheritance taxation may have been appropriate in the early stages of the movement; but for the future they are hopelessly crude and inadequate.

The levies in question (to repeat) are mainly in the nature of *ad rem* charges. They have merit as against many other taxes; for they do mitigate inequality by modifying, however unsystematically and inelegantly, one phase of existing property rights. But they cannot pretend to fairness among persons. This shortcoming is widely recognized in the case of estate taxes—which may be regarded as a device for rescuing some revenue potentialities from the sentimentality of legislatures. But the inheritance-tax form, while better, is not much better. Inheritance taxes take no account of the prior circumstances of the beneficiary; moreover, they are levied progressively not according to the total of property inherited but according to the size of each transfer separately.

Until recently, the whole system of levies in the United States could be regarded mainly as a penalty on those whose benefactors failed to pass down their property before death. That any revenues were forthcoming is presumably attributable to untimely deaths, to utter distrust of beneficiaries, or to mere disregard of their interests. With the gift taxes, we have recognized an anomaly and made a start toward dealing with it. To date, however, we have only imposed a small obstacle to avoidance, established a slight charge for the privilege of escaping tax, and created a fine market for a special kind of legal and financial services.

The cumulative features of our federal gifts tax are an interesting novelty; but this levy falls far short of preventing systematic avoidance. There is the unaccountable differentiation of rates between the gifts and estates taxes; there is the excessive specific exemption ($5,000) of particular transfers; and there is the failure to coordinate the two levies, by making the rates of estates tax dependent on the amounts transferred by gift—not to mention the enormous exemptions and the trivial initial rates under both these levies.

The more obvious structural defects of these complementary taxes might easily be corrected. With slight revision of existing legislation, we might obtain a combination of levies which would impose approximately the same total taxes on every person and his estate regardless of how his distributions were divided between gifts *inter vivos* and transfers at death. However, we should then have merely a progressive tax upon persons according to the total amount of property distributed. Such a tax would be more productive and less arbitrary than earlier levies of its kind; but it would have little to commend it on grounds of equity; it would savor excessively of a progressive penalty upon saving; and, with really effective application of an unsatisfactory principle, the inherent faults of this form of levy might become critical.

The corresponding reconstruction of our inheritance taxes is more forbidding in its complexity. It would be necessary to rebuild them into a personal levy (or levies) corresponding to the federal gift tax on donors, covering both gifts and inheritances, giving each beneficiary a once-and-for-all exemption, and taxing him with respect to each receipt according to the total previously received. The total amounts paid by a beneficiary might then be approximately the same, regardless of the number of distributions in which he participated or of their distribution in time. Inheritance taxation, developing along such lines, might come to make some sense; but, again, what should we have after all the necessary legislation? Even apart from administrative difficulties, the picture is still very unattractive.

If, after removal of obvious anomalies, legislation did apply the essential principle of inheritance taxation, we should then have a separate personal levy, progressive according to the total of those particular receipts which (for purposes of justice) an irrelevant legal criterion establishes to be gifts, inheritances, and bequests. In such a tax one finds all the shortcomings of the "analytic" income tax. To provide appropriate company for it in the tax system, we should have a progressive personal tax with respect to wages and salaries, another with respect to ground rents, another with respect to interest, dividends, and business profits, another with respect to capital gains, etc.!

Thus, to make a somewhat sensible system out of existing death duties would require elaborate and extensive reconstruction; and the possible results, at best, fail to warrant much enthusiasm about the undertaking. Reconstruction along the lines of our proposal for broadening the income-tax base seems hardly more difficult to carry out and far more satisfying in terms of its probable effects. The income tax would become more equitable among persons; the tax base would become conceptually simpler and more objective; errors and uncertainties of assessment would, because of prospective counteraction later on, become less serious; the diseconomies involved in the elaborate and devious business of tax avoidance would be diminished; and the treasury would be placed in a position to require full accounting by taxpayers for every acquisition and disposition of property. With complementary arrangements to be noted later on, we should have a system full of internal checks, with provision for wholesale cancellation of errors automatically, and with a minimum of opportunities for successful falsifying of returns. These special virtues and potentialities of the income-tax device are of immense practical importance and deserve to be carefully exploited.

Our proposals regarding gratuitous receipts will encounter the familiar complaint about double taxation which, though meaningless in itself, may suggest some difficulties. Our general argument, of course, has anticipated this objection. Income taxes are levies upon persons, not upon parts of the social income; their proper objective is that of imposing equitable relative levies upon individuals, not that of reaching somehow every item of income. Considerations of equity surely afford little ground for excluding (or including) particular receipts according to the intentions of second parties. Gifts are very much like earnings, and earnings are often quite like gifts. The whole return from property is, in a sense, a gift from the community. Where money is earned by common labor, the distinction may be fairly clear; but many remunerative employments only require people's doing what they would quite enjoy doing without compensation. If it is impractical to graduate taxes according to the pleasure return from one's earning activity, surely it is hard to defend exclusion of certain receipts merely because one has done nothing or given nothing in return. Thus, as regards donees, current income-tax practices as to gifts find no sanction in considerations of fairness; and they do involve a distinction between gifts and compensation which introduces serious administrative difficulties and which, moreover, invites the dressing-up of real exchanges in the guise of one-sided transfers. On the other hand, it may be argued that the arrangements which we have proposed would fall well short of fairness as regards donors. This point we shall return to shortly.

It would obviously be folly for an income tax to try to reach all gifts. It is unthinkable that taxpayers should be obliged to account in their returns for the value of all dinners and entertainments which they enjoy as guests, and even for cigars and "lifts"—to use more of Kleinwächter's examples. Besides the overwhelming administrative difficulties, one faces here all the problems of the *Flügeladjutant*. How should one value things obtained by gift which one would never purchase for one's self. What is the pecuniary equivalent of a Corona-Corona to a poor pedagog? As a practical matter, of course, these problems may be dismissed on the ground that such receipts, in the main, are paid for, as a matter of the social amenities, except as they accrue to persons who would pay little or no income tax in any event.

But, if we cannot include all gifts, we must face the necessity of drawing a definite line somewhere—and the danger that any line may produce both unfortunate discrimination and loopholes for deliberate evasion. It seems a minimum requirement that all receipts in the form of real estate and other investment assets should be included. Perhaps legislation also should specify major items of consumer capital, such as yachts, motorcars, and valuable art objects, and then add "all other gifts of property" (excluding trifles), with a small annual exemption (say, $200) with respect to this miscellaneous category or catch-all provision.

Difficult questions arise here with regard to the family. Where adults reside within the household of a benefactor, our general rules would call for assessing them with respect to their share of the consumption expenses of the household. The appropriate measures are forbidding from the standpoint of administration; and we may be reconciled to the ignoring of gifts in many such cases. To do this, however, would sometimes discriminate seriously against those whose living was provided wholly or partly by their benefactor outside his household (i.e., by cash contributions). In any event, the question of principle remains. Our scheme would require that beneficiaries be taxed with respect to gifts, without deductions on the part of the donors. The charge of double counting merely begs the question. But is the scheme grossly unfair to those who contribute to the support of others?

It is a common criticism of our existing income taxes that they differentiate meagerly, especially within the upper income classes, between families of different size.[3] Suppose that Mr. A and Mr. B have annual incomes of $100,000 each. Both are married; but Mr. A has no dependents except his wife, while Mr. B maintains a household including his wife, five children, and three aged relatives. Now the difference in the federal income taxes paid by these two gentlemen amounted, until recently, merely to the normal tax on the $3,200 credit ($400 each) for the eight additional dependents— or to less than 1 per cent of the total tax. The difference is now larger (about 6 per cent), since the credits apply also for surtax; but it still seems unduly small.

Approaching the matter from this angle, one is tempted to urge substantial concessions in the cases of taxpayers who support numerous dependents. It seems reasonable enough that the credits for, at least, minor dependents should vary directly with the family income. This might be arranged—as indeed was done under the German *Reichseinkommensteuer*—by providing minimum and maximum credits per child, together with a credit expressed as a percentage of income between those limits. It may also seem reasonable that adult members of a taxpayer's household should be taxed with respect to that part of the joint consumption expenses attributable to them (less contributions by them), with deduction of the amounts so imputed in determining the taxable income of the householder. Consistency, of course, would require the authorization of generous deductions

[3] See *Report of the Committee on National Debt and Taxation* (Cmd. 2800), (London, 1927), paragraphs 358 and 1014.

with respect to amounts contributed to the support of persons outside the household.

Some concessions of this sort seem necessary to equitable relative taxation of persons with similar earnings and different family obligations. To commend them, at any rate, is to raise question as to the merits of our proposal for the "double taxation" of gifts. Such concessions, of course, would serve both to reduce the total yield of our more equitable taxes and to diminish the effective degree of progression. While these effects might be avoided by appropriate alteration of rates, it is highly unlikely that compensating rate differences would be forthcoming. To rest one's case on such considerations, however, would be inappropriate.

Personal taxation, we argue, should seek to minimize inequities among persons, but subject always to a requirement of simplicity and definiteness in the underlying rules. The best guide for policy is the principle that income taxes should diminish systematically an objectively measurable kind of inequality. Now, in the case before us, it can hardly be seriously proposed that donors be permitted to deduct all gifts for purposes of income tax; such a proposal would repudiate the very idea of inheritance taxation. Moreover, unless all gifts are to be deductible, there is a presumption against permitting deduction for any of them. Including some and excluding others, one must draw a line of distinction; and there appear to be no clear and simple principles which could be followed in fixing such a line.

Thus, one faces the choice between following a rule in spite of its occasionally unfortunate consequences and, on the other hand, admitting a mass of casuistic distinctions and exceptions. Stressing the view that the levy must be fair among persons, one inclines toward the latter choice. This view can never be ignored; and it usually guides one well through particular issues. But it must never be trusted implicitly or permitted the status of a court of last resort. Otherwise, one removes the whole inquiry to a world of dialectic populated only by doctrines of ability, faculty, sacrifice, maximum social advantage, and their kind; and from this realm there is no bridge back to a real world of tax legislation and administration. The criterion of equity, by itself, leads only to a vague and elusive ideal, not to a sound and workable income tax. Indeed, it leads away from income entirely or (what is the same) to casuistic definition. So, one must face the fact that income is an actual tax base and that income taxes must finally be appraised in terms of general rules of procedure which best define their nature. Hence arises the need for rigorous, objective definition.

Our preference in this instance is for following the general rule, closely if not relentlessly, i.e., for rather straightforward taxation of persons according to their periodic accretions of means, and with relatively little regard for the manner in which the means are employed. One may persevere stubbornly in the contention that, as a matter of principle, gifts are consumption to the donor and therefore not properly deductible. They are not expenses of acquiring "income" (although some contributions of business firms are largely of this nature), and they are not capital losses. Broadly they represent merely personal expenditure. It may seem evasive to invoke such highly formal distinctions; admittedly, the obligation to support an aged relative may not be very different from that of paying one's creditors. But rather empty distinctions are frequently necessary to definiteness and objectivity. Besides, a merely legal difference will often involve important psychological differences too. There are consumption incidents to charity and generosity which are meagerly paralleled in the payment of debts. The person who can and does support his destitute relatives is surely better off himself on that account than one who, helpless, must endure the spectacle of their distress. As regards minor dependents, it would be hard to maintain that the raising of children is not a form of consumption on the part of parents—whether one believes in the subsidizing of such consumption or not. Individuals have, at the extremes, widely different consumption requirements—medical attention, recreation, servants, transportation, etc.—which no workable income tax can allow for adequately; and people who need much to keep alive at all are better off with large incomes than with small ones, as are those with numerous dependents.

After all, we are faced with an excessive inequality of economic power and with a kind of inequality which bears no significant relation to the inequalities in needs. So, it may suffice to attack economic inequality directly, to diminish it as it stands, without trying much to twist it toward a kind of inequality which our sentiments may approve; otherwise, our main objective may be lost in the pursuit of ill-defined and less important ends. The

income tax is not a proper vehicle for sumptuary legislation. Besides, there is something wrong with a system
which gives great power to a few people, no matter how
they use that power. If a man devotes practically all
of his million-dollar income to the support of the most
worthy causes, the question remains of whether anyone
should be permitted so much power. Having a large income, moreover, will often be the cause of one's having
many dependents. If capable people are maintained in
useless activities by the generosity of prosperous relatives, that is a conspicuously unwelcome consequence of
inequality with which intelligent policy should reckon.
If the training of a few children is made the object of
expenditures involving a disproportionate share of the
community's resources, that again is something which
the rules of the game should not encourage.

None of this argument implies disapproval of small,
fixed credits with respect to minor children or others
who are incapable of self-support and are, in fact, primarily dependent on the particular taxpayer. Small and
foolproof concessions of the kind now commonly made
are not incompatible with reasonably close adherence
to simple general rules. On the other hand, it seems
doubtful whether they could wisely or safely be extended
along the lines suggested by the Colwyn Committee.[4]

Any scheme of the kind here proposed, like any
scheme of inheritance taxation, must fall short of perfection, since it is impossible to include all gifts or inheritances in the form of special training, education, and
social position. This is a major kind of inheritance, es-

[4] See above, n. 3.

pecially in middle-class families; but it assumes no definite or measurable form and must largely be disregarded for taxation purposes. If the omission involves some inequities and some deliberate avoidance, there are at least some happy effects; and there may be useful counteraction of imperfections elsewhere in the system. First, we may recall that the law does not and presumably cannot wisely permit depreciation deductions with respect to investment in personal earning capacity. Second, the failure to reach the items in question as receipts of the beneficiaries may compensate in some measure for the niggardliness of allowances with respect to dependents.

Should there be generous special exemptions for widows and direct heirs? One might argue that the criterion of gain itself calls for generosity here, since such beneficiaries are only realizing on an equity which was there before the transfer. This point, however, is not well taken, for the equity must have arisen sometime, even though it date back to the beneficiary's birth. Thus, the transfer can be regarded as a realization of gains which, if imputable to earlier years, were not previously recognized for purposes of the tax. The argument, however, may support some concessions, by way of permission to spread the receipts over several tax years, or by way of rebates under an averaging scheme (see below, chap. vii). As a matter of practical politics, and of justice, some special exemptions might well be conceded for widows and other dependents incapable of self-support but not for direct heirs as such. On the other hand, the fact that few widows and dependents ever inherit anything at all should dictate narrow limitation of such concessions.[5]

It remains now to note that the treatment of gratuitous receipts as taxable income, while clearly preferable to inheritance taxation as it stands, would fail to capture some of the virtues of inheritance taxation in its ideal form—i.e., in the form of the cumulative personal tax on beneficiaries. As against such a levy, our inclusive levy on annual income would impose relatively inadequate total taxes with respect to large transfers which

[5] A good case can be made for quite generous treatment of widows and widowers, provided the special concessions can be protected against abuse. Special treatment is obviously appropriate where the wife has, in fact, contributed substantially toward accumulation of the property which she obtains as a bequest or inheritance—and perhaps in all cases with respect to property accumulated during the marriage period. But there is obviously a problem of meeting such dictates of fairness within a system of simple and workable rules and, in particular, of avoiding abuses like those which have occurred in connection with federal pensions. It might suffice, granting generous exemptions, to deny the exemption where the wife was much younger than the husband, or to scale it down according to the age discrepancy or (inversely) according to the duration of the marriage relationship. Moreover, the exemptions for minor children (which properly might vary inversely according to their ages) might well be added to the widow's exemption in cases where the children are not provided for separately.

Adequate discussion of the issues involved here would be out of proportion in this chapter. It may be possible to devise sound schemes for larger differentiation among taxpayers according to their needs and for larger recognition of the family or household as the unit for progressive taxation. The writer, while disposed to examine concrete proposals sympathetically, is very skeptical about the practical possibilities. Administrative difficulties and dangers of excessive avoidance opportunities loom large. Moreover, the differentiation in question seems unimportant at the top of the income scale; and, with respect to middle-class taxpayers, it is likely to involve heavy losses of revenues which, in fact, must be made good by taxes involving more undesirable effects than those which the differentiation might mitigate. It seems unwise to stress the need for larger differentiation in the lower income-tax brackets until the effective rates of tax are vastly different from those now imposed.

were carried out very gradually. Thus our proposals, while calling for drastic change in existing death duties, do not call for abandonment of the old forms of levy. The case for the taxation of gratuitous receipts as income stands, as does the case for regarding the income tax as the basic form of levy upon inheritance; but the case for supplementary levies is also strong. The accumulation of property through receipt of gifts, inheritances, and bequests is a kind of accumulation which can be taxed with least adverse effect upon the morale of an enterprise economy; and opinion generally supports especially heavy taxation of "income" in this form. So, just as one might argue for some relief to the taxpayer whose inheritance is concentrated in a single year, one may also argue for a supplementary tax which would diminish or remove the advantages of steady, gradual, and long-continued transfer. Not least of the merits of such arrangements is that they serve to minimize the influence of taxation itself upon people's practices in the management and disposition of their property, and to minimize the business of specialists in tax avoidance.

The appropriate arrangements here would take the form of a cumulative personal tax on beneficiaries with respect to gifts, inheritances, and bequests (after the manner of the existing federal gift tax on donors), with a credit for all amounts paid as personal income tax by virtue of the inclusion of such receipts—i.e., with a credit for the difference between what one's income-tax payments actually were and what they would have been without the receipts in question. Such a levy, together with an inclusive income tax, would afford something very close to the ideal structural basis for personal taxa-

tion. Incidentally, a good case might be made for retention (and consolidation) of our federal taxes on estates
and gifts, with lower exemptions and with very low
rates, because of the value of the returns in the administration of other levies.

This proposed supplementary levy again raises difficult practical questions with respect to gifts in kind.
Our present federal tax is confined to gifts of property.
Now in cases where adult sons and daughters are supported entirely by their parents, any income of their
own, from property or salaries, may be devoted largely
to accumulation. In such cases, considerations of equity
would recognize no difference between actual gifts of
property and additional accumulations attributable to
the gratuitous receipt of living expenses. This imper-
fection, to be sure, is not impressive, in a tax with the
rates and exemptions of our present gift tax, and with the
extravagant specific exemption of $5,000; but it might
loom large in a levy which was more than a decorative
element in the system.

This problem might be dealt with, as regards minors,
by making their total property holdings taxable under
this supplementary tax when they attain majority, with
a credit for the total of income taxes previously paid by
or on behalf of the minor. The income tax might continue as it is under present arrangements; but the supplementary levy would be postponed, as it were, until
the child becomes of age. There would then be no distinction, for this tax, between accumulation by gift or
inheritance and accumulation by minors from their own
income. Similar arrangements might be extended, of
course, to all adults as well, making net accumulation

the basis of the tax in all cases. But a levy on accumulation, while reasonable and expedient for the period of minority, is hardly to be commended generally. With it, we should lose the essential rationale of inheritance taxation—not to mention the unreasonable discrimination against saving and the untoward economic effects. The purpose of the supplementary levy is that of controlling inheritance. So, for adults it must distinguish sharply between property acquired through saving and property acquired from others. But this distinction breaks down where the taxpayer's consumption expenses are covered wholly or largely by parents or other benefactors, unless this item of receipts is reached under the supplementary tax. While these receipts in kind should be reached for income tax as well, the credit arrangement would make that unnecessary—unless easy reconciliation of returns under the two levies were desirable for administrative reasons.

To attempt to reach all such gifts would hardly be feasible. However, it should not be impractical to employ rules which would require that they be accounted for in all cases where the omission might be serious. Thus, such receipts might be ignored in all cases where "other taxable income" fell below, say, $5,000 and/or where the items in question would amount to less than $1,000. If the reporting involved much inconvenience, this might lead to nominal separation of households and to substitution of straightforward cash contribution—which would minimize difficulties all around. For administration the number of cases involved would be relatively small in any event. On the other hand, one may have misgivings about the wisdom of introducing a double incentive for the making of contributions in the guise of compensation for services. In any case, the underlying difficulties are not peculiar to the scheme which we are proposing.[6]

[6] In passing, we may mention an interesting anomaly in our federal income tax with respect to gifts. Under the earlier laws the basis for calculating gain or loss from the sale of property acquired by gift was the same for the donee as for the (original) donor. Thus, persons receiving by gift property which has depreciated greatly since its purchase by the donor acquired not only the property but also a valuable potential deduction from taxable income. This situation has been corrected partially. The 1934 Act provides that gains shall be calculated on the same basis as if the property had remained in the hands of the donor; but that losses shall be calculated on that basis *or* on the basis of the value of the property at the time of transfer by gift, whichever is lower. Thus, the anomaly remains. The property acquired is not taxed as income; but, if it is subsequently sold for less than its estimated value when acquired, the "loss" may be used to reduce the donee's income tax.

A similar anomaly appears in the new legislation regarding capital gains and losses. The *Report of the Joint Committee on Internal Revenue Taxation* (I, Part VII, 3 and 20–21)—from which the present sec. 117 was adapted in principle—recommended that the percentage of capital gain or loss to be included in or deducted from taxable income should be determined, in the case of assets acquired by gift, only on the basis of the time during which the property was actually held by the donee (that the period should be determined from the time of gift, not from the time of purchase by the donor). Congress, however, did not see fit to accept this suggestion. While suggested with the thought of withholding in part the concessions of the new scheme from donees (and thus wisely), such a provision would have been very convenient for donees who acquired potential deductible "losses." It is interesting that the report, while dealing with this whole problem, raised no question as to the *basis* for calculating gain or loss—even specified retention of the old arrangements on that score.

The whole situation here illustrates how unsubstantial an apparent consistency can be. It may seem reasonable to maintain a parallelism between the provisions for calculating gains and those for calculating losses—even though it is sheer foolishness. On the gains side, everything can be said for the present arrangement, as a means for preventing evasion through transfer of property which has appreciated. But there can be no question of inconsistency if one, supporting the provisions as to gains, insists that no valid excuse can be offered for allowing persons to deduct "losses" of any kind on property acquired by gift. If the gift were taxable to the donee, the situation would be entirely different—and the prevailing arrangements as to subsequent gains and losses, entirely sensible.

CHAPTER VII

CAPITAL GAINS

GAINS and losses from transactions in investment assets present one of the most prominent and most controversial issues of income taxation. The problem has left its imprint upon the whole literature of income definition. It has been dealt with in strikingly different ways under different tax laws. Moreover, there is no clear basis in principle for the practices actually followed anywhere—and little inclination, on the part of competent students, to approve or defend the existing arrangements. In England, capital gains, except in the case of professional speculators, are regarded as "mere accretions of capital" and, along with other "casual profits," are excluded from the tax base. The French law is substantially the same; but the tax is said to be utterly ineffective as regards speculative profits.[1]

---

[1] For admirable description and criticism of the English, French, and German practices see R. M. Haig, "Taxation of Capital Gains," a series of six articles in the *Wall Street Journal*, beginning in the issue of March 23, 1937 (March 23, 25, 29; April 2, 8, 13). Concluding his discussion of the situation in England, Haig says:

"It has been shown: (1) that the exemption of capital gains in England is far more narrow than it is commonly conceived to be; (2) that the partial exemption of capital gains under their law involves drawing an arbitrary line between taxable and exempt transactions, with uncertain and inequitable results as between individuals in substantially similar circumstances; (3) that the British themselves are far from satisfied with their formula, a Royal Commission having gone so far as to declare that 'it cannot be justified'; (4) that the formula places a premium on the transformation of taxable income into exempt capital gains, a premium sufficiently substantial to give rise to tax

In Germany, an attempt is made to distinguish, by means of simple and arbitrary rules, between the gains of speculators and the gains of investors.[2] In the United States, our federal law taxed capital gains like other income prior to 1921; but since that time they have been accorded very special treatment, under curiously arbitrary provisions.

In all these countries there is marked dissatisfaction with prevailing legislation. Competent English students

avoidance and loss of revenue in spite of England's superior administration and her high degree of taxpayer cooperation; and (5) that the devices for tax avoidance cause investors to buy and sell securities at 'unnatural' times, with consequences for the market that may be expected to be accentuated under American conditions."

In this connection we may also refer to the illuminationg section on the English law in Roswell Magill, *Taxable Income* (New York, 1936), pp. 70–90, and to the following paragraph in particular (pp. 88–89):

"Viewing the English cases as a whole, it appears that the limitation of the taxation of the profits on sales to sales made in the trade or business of the taxpayer gives rise to difficult questions of fact in borderline cases. The question largely turns on the intent of the taxpayer, as indicated objectively or even subjectively. Intent may be determined from the character of the commodity sold, the nature of the taxpayer's ordinary activities, the number of transactions in the commodity in question. In view of the inherent difficulty of determining questions of intent, and of the fact that in these particular cases the question is essentially one of degree, it is surprising that there are not more litigated cases in the British reports."

[2] The *Reichseinkommensteuer* of 1920 followed quite closely the radical proposals of Professor Schanz and his followers; but it was promptly repealed. Subsequent legislation was modeled more closely along the lines of the earlier Prussian tax and, as regards capital gains, was essentially similar to the English law. The sharp rule-of-thumb distinctions were first introduced in 1925; the legislation of that year exempted in effect all profits from the sale of securities held over three months, and all profits from the sale of real estate held over two years. In 1934, profits from the sale of bonds were exempted outright; but the exemption with respect to profits from the sale of other securities was narrowed, the period being increased from three months to one year (see Haig, *loc. cit.*).

are recommending changes which would broaden the tax base and undermine the traditional exemption of casual profits. Changes in this direction with respect to capital gains were proposed and indorsed by the Royal Commission in 1920. The vigorous writing of men like Schanz, Pistorius, Moll, and Popitz in Germany displays no animus more clearly than that of opposition to exemption of speculative profits under the *Reichseinkommensteuer*. In the United States everyone condemns the capital-gain provisions. A small, or very inarticulate, minority deplores their regressive character and feels that capital profits should receive no special favors. Another group, whose servants are legion and whose grievances are always "news," is persuaded that any taxation of such gains under income tax is an insufferable abomination. Here, as elsewhere, the displeasure of paying for government is rationalized into opposition to certain levies on the basis of considerations which would be noble if they were relevant. The common contention is that the capital-gain provisions lead to momentous diseconomies through interference with orderly marketing of property. Latterly some persons have gone so far as to elevate these provisions into the front rank among causes of business, or at least stock-market, crises and cycles.

It does seem thoroughly unsound, as a matter of definition, to set up a category of capital profits outside (or even within) the income concept. Although no satisfactory line can be drawn between these and other gains, and although any separation violates the underlying principle of income taxation, still it is not surprising that an issue should be found here. The case of capital gains reveals most strikingly those shortcomings of income tax which arise from instability of the *numéraire*. Moreover, such speculative profits invite special attention because of their peculiarly unstable, irregular, and fortuitous character.

The irregularity of personal income presents a real problem for equitable taxation and one of special relevance here. Any tax graduated according to income for single years must impose undue burden upon persons with widely fluctuating incomes. Where the fluctuation arises from windfalls and gratuities, the discrimination may be unobjectionable, for heavy levies upon such receipts are generally approved. The same feeling as to capital gains is, however, surely less common, for they have at least some flavor of "earnings." Besides, losses fluctuate as well as gains, thus aggravating the situation.

To eliminate both capital gains and losses in computing taxable income, however, would simply prohibit fairness in relative levies among persons. To do this, or even to make the more moderate concessions of our federal law, is to undermine the very basis of income taxation. Proponents of such measures would have us go but a little way toward modifying the penalty of progression upon irregularity, at the cost of abandoning effort to reach individuals according to their relative income circumstances. They would persist in the attempt to treat income taxes as *ad rem* levies—an error less serious, by the way, with respect to the English tax of the last century. It should require little insight to appreciate the folly of allowing for irregularity of personal income through exemption, or special treatment, of particular kinds of receipts. The income tax is properly a tax upon persons according to income; and it loses something of its *raison d'être* whenever distinction is made among kinds of "income," gains, or receipts. Moreover, special treatment of certain kinds of gains or receipts goes a very small way toward reducing irregularity of personal income; and, in this instance, it displays solicitude for a small group whose "rights" are properly not an object of serious concern.

Any special treatment of capital gains per se also requires introduction into the law of arbitrary, unsatisfactory, and unnecessary distinctions. In America we say that "capital assets" shall mean property other than "stock in trade." Gain or loss from the sale of such assets is capital gain or loss. Strikingly similar are the definitions of the *Reichseinkommensteuer*. The English inspector (and courts) must decide whether the transactions in question are a part of the taxpayer's ordinary business—whether they have to do with vocation or avocation! That such definitions must lead to strange results from the viewpoint of equity is immediately obvious; that their mitigation of tax inequities which arise from income-instability is pitifully meager, seems also beyond argument. Nor do they simplify the task of administration.

Special treatment of capital gains is especially objectionable for the opportunities which it provides for deliberate evasion or avoidance. It might well stimulate issue of bonds at low nominal rates and heavy discount —or at least lead to concentration of such issues in the hands of persons subject to the higher rates of tax. Companies might even find it advantageous to issue bonds without annual interest, for investors liquidating in advance of maturity could claim the blessings of section 117. Furthermore, one sees here important incentive to restriction of corporate dividends or to infrequent distribution—which would permit substantial avoidance if stockholders were to liquidate in advance of distributions. With the rise of specialized investment trusts, the possibilities here are of no small proportions. "Convert your income into capital gains" may well become a potent slogan for security salesmen of the future.

The case in favor of some allowance for the irregularity of taxable income, however, is strong, for prevailing methods of measurement do aggravate the inequities. The real culprit here is the realization criterion. Gains and losses from capital transactions are recognized only when the investor "gets out." One may complain of this practice; but to demand that it be abandoned outright is to display little regard for practical considerations. Escape from it is possible in the case of actively traded securities; but, unfortunately, the realization criterion must be accepted as a practical necessity. What, then, can be done to provide the desired relief?

It requires some temerity to propose additional administrative complications. Yet relief can perhaps be provided for highly unstable incomes without serious imposition on the treasury. Would it not be possible to introduce some modification of the averaging system? The earlier English procedure under Schedule D had appeal even for those who urged its abandonment; and it seems that something may well be salvaged from it for the future. A specific proposal may at least suggest possibilities.

Let each individual be taxed annually as heretofore. Then, say in 1940, let him compute his average taxable income for the years 1935–39, inclusive. Next, let him compute what his total taxes would have been if his average income had been his actual income for each year. Then, if this amount is less than the total of his five actual payments by more than 10 per cent, let him claim rebate for the excess over 10 per cent. The percentage margin is introduced to keep the number of claims within reason—though apology might be made on broader grounds; and the exact figure should be fixed with regard to questions of administrative cost. The period chosen is likewise arbitrary. If it be very long, relief will come too tardily. If it be very short, the average loses significance and the number of claims is needlessly increased. Considerations of simplicity also argue for the use of fixed periods, opportunity to file claims being granted simultaneously to all taxpayers, say, every fifth year.

That such abatement is preferable to special treatment for especially unstable kinds or elements of "income" is manifest. Capital gains are now accorded special treatment even where they serve to stabilize taxable income; and the widest fluctuation, wherein no capital gains appear, occasions no relief. All these anomalies would disappear under the provisions we have proposed. And no serious problem of administration is apparent. Methods of calculating the tax base are unaltered, and no additional data are required. All the claims for a period could be handled by a few persons with calculating machines.

The fact that capital gains and losses are often and largely fictitious suggests a problem to which we have referred in an earlier chapter. It remains now to point out that the difficulties are at least as great for practice as for theory. Considerations of justice demand that changes in monetary conditions be taken into account in the measurement of gain and loss. As soon as one begins to translate this generalization into actual procedures, however, one comes quickly to the conviction that some things are well let alone.

It would be necessary to employ index numbers. Presumably, definite methods of calculation would have to be prescribed in the statute. Indexes would have to be calculated far into the past. The time of purchase would have to be ascertained for each asset sold. Where large gain appeared, it would have to be corrected by the appropriate relatives. Where the nominal gain was small, correction might show loss; and surely losses should be allowed where the investor nominally came out even. Such would be the case for periods of increasing price level. During periods of falling prices nominal gains would have to be corrected by additions, no-gain transactions made to show profits, and nominal losses converted into gains.

Yet even such elaborate adjustments would be meager indeed. If prices were rising, the person who disposed of his capital assets would be unduly favored as against him who continued to use them in his business. In justice to the latter, he should be allowed to write up his assets for purposes of future depreciation charges. The whole scheme becomes practically absurd when we turn to the opposite case and recognize that, with falling prices, it would be necessary to limit total depreciation charges to amounts far below original cost.

It thus seems the part of wisdom to abandon hope of correcting for instability through special income-tax devices. Persons interested in equitable taxation will do well to join in the crusade for stable monetary conditions and in prayer for some intelligence in the regulation of financial institutions. However, it may be comforting to recognize that there is a sort of compensation in these inequities of income tax. Those hardest hit by taxation of fictitious gains will be, in the main, not those who have suffered in other ways from the depreciation of money. Indeed, they will still be far better off than those whose property has been in the form of bonds, mortgages, and annuities. Taxation of fictitious gains, therefore, may serve to produce a not inequitable counterredistribution of income and property. On the other hand, the deduction of nominal losses during periods of falling prices may serve ultimately to transfer some of the tax burden to those classes which have gained most from money appreciation. Furthermore, some scheme of rebating or abatement for taxpayers whose year-to-year income has been highly irregular (like that suggested above) would mitigate considerably the inequities of levy on merely nominal gains or profits.

It is frequently argued that the treasury loses more through the deduction of capital losses than it gains through inclusion of capital profits and, therefore, that the disregard of both gains and losses on capital assets is desirable merely on revenue grounds. The facts here have not been studied carefully (and no statistical study could tell us much), but there is a presumption of factual accuracy in the contention. To a considerable extent, taxpayers will deliberately realize losses, and avoid realization of gains, out of regard for effects on their income-tax obligations.[3]

This "maximum revenue criterion," however, deserves little consideration. An income tax would obviously yield more revenue, with the same rates, if it were based on gross rather than on net income; but few people would find this consideration decisive in favor of the former type of levy. It is the main purpose of the income tax to secure an equitable, progressive distribution of tax burdens among individuals; and the tax will hardly serve well to that end if its detailed provisions are designed to maximize the revenue obtained from a given structure of rates and exemptions. The main and decisive case for inclusion of capital items rests on the fact that equity among individuals is impossible under an income tax which disregards such items of gain and loss—not to mention the presumption against arbitrary distinctions and casuistic definition of the tax base.

The practical problem here, by the way, is primarily one which has to do with the corporation and undistributed corporate earnings.[4] Capital gains and losses,

[3] In large measure, these opportunities for tax avoidance arise out of glaring and correctable faults in the law (see below), not merely out of the practice of taxing capital gains.

[4] It has been estimated that 85 per cent of capital gains arise out of sales of securities (*Reports to the Joint Committee on Internal Revenue Taxation*, I. Part VII, 14).

to be sure, are not confined to transactions in securities; and considerable inequity must arise in the relative taxation of different persons if gains and losses on other forms of property are not brought into the tax base. The real problem, however, is one of deliberate evasion; and it is only through corporations that special treatment of capital gains opens the way to easy, systematic avoidance of personal income tax on a large scale.

The American income-tax system, as a basis for equitable, progressive levies, is inferior at many points to income taxes abroad. Indeed, one may say that only in its provisions as to capital gains and losses is it in advance of practices in other countries. In the beginning such gains and losses were taxable and deductible, when realized, just like any other gains and losses. During the early twenties our law was revised, through arbitrary limitations with respect to capital items, in the direction of the inferior practices of the English and German taxes. Recent legislation, however, seems to move in the opposite direction. Section 117 of the Revenue Act of 1934, while leaving us still far from a satisfactory solution, does at least correct some of the grosser mistakes of earlier laws.

After the war it was commonly argued that our income tax was interfering seriously with the orderly marketing of capital assets. While it is hard to find substantial point in this contention, it is not surprising that Congress responded to the demand for concessions as to capital gains. The rates of tax were extremely high; speculative profits were enormous and were, in large measure, merely nominal gains from wartime inflation;

and the main burden of the high surtaxes was attributable to a feature of our law which was novel and unsupported by precedent abroad.

Beginning with the Act of 1921, the law provided that inclusion of capital gains should not increase one's income tax by more than $12\frac{1}{2}$ per cent of the gain. In the upper brackets this represented an enormous concession, under the surtax rates then prevailing—and a concession which afterward varied widely with changes in the surtax rates. In the Act of 1924 there appears for the first time the nominally consistent provision regarding capital losses, whereby it was provided that the deduction of capital losses should not reduce one's tax by more than $12\frac{1}{2}$ per cent of the loss.

These arrangements, which prevailed until the Act of 1934, had little to commend them. They introduced into the law an arbitrary, antiprogressive element and a concession which was confined to the highest income brackets. The person whose annual income, including realized capital gains, never reached into brackets carrying a rate as high as $12\frac{1}{2}$ per cent was not benefited at all; and those in the highest brackets gained progressively according to the size of their incomes.

Even the apparent symmetry between the provisions as to gains and losses was empty and illusory. There was consistency only from the viewpoint of the treasury —i.e., in terms of the spurious "revenue criterion." To the extent that the people realizing losses are not the ones who at other times report the large gains (or not in similar amounts), the relative inequities involved in limiting the taxes on certain types of gains are only aggravated and increased by the limitation of loss deductions. It is not enough that the provisions should be approximately offsetting in the typical or modal case or on the average. There can be little reason for limiting loss deductions for some taxpayers because others have enjoyed concessions as to capital gains; and the inequity seems the more striking when we consider that the gains will ordinarily be associated with large, and the losses with small, incomes "from other sources."

Under the 1934 law the method of dealing with capital gains is entirely changed, and the amount of the special concession in the upper brackets has been considerably reduced. Under section 117 the taxpayer is required to report as taxable income only a percentage of his gain from the sale of a capital asset, the percentage varying according to how long the asset has been held. One hundred per cent of the gain is to be reported if the asset has been held for not more than one year; 80 per cent, if it has been held more than one year but not more than two years; 60 per cent, if it has been held for more than two, but not more than five, years; 40 per cent, if it has been held for more than five, but not more than ten, years; and 30 per cent, if it has been held more than ten years. The same percentage scale must be applied in the deduction of all capital losses.

This general scheme was proposed in a report made in 1929 to the Joint Committee on Internal Revenue Taxation by its Division of Investigation. The scale of percentages suggested in the report was slightly higher than that of the present law; but, on the other hand, the report proposed outright exemption of gains (and disregard of losses) on property held over fifteen years. The recommendations purport to be based on the excellent principle that capital gains ought so to be taxed that individuals will pay approximately what they would have paid if the accrued appreciation, calculated at a uniform rate of accrual, had been added to their taxable income each year during the period for which the asset was held. In the report it is shown that, at 1928 rates, the proposed scheme would produce approximately that result in the cases of taxpayers whose only income, above the exemptions, is derived from capital gains![5] Certainly the fact that the scheme would work reasonably well in such special cases is a small recommendation.

Here again one sees, in the *Report* and in the provisions of the present law, the unfortunate consequences of introducing *ad rem* elements into a personal tax. An important step forward has been made, to be sure, in mitigating the antiprogressive character of the capital-gains section; but there has been only mitigation. The new provisions do extend some concessions with respect to capital profits to taxpayers in the lower-income brackets. On the other hand, they retain concessions at the upper-income levels where, according to the criterion proposed, concessions are unwarranted. In the case of the largest taxpayers, it makes no difference (apart from rate changes) how capital gains are distributed in time. The person whose income is always high enough to make him subject to the maximum rate suffers no penalty

[5] Even according to these calculations, however, the scheme works unduly to the advantage of persons with the larger capital gains (see *ibid.*, p. 24).

whatever, under progression, from wide fluctuations in his year-to-year income. But such persons, under the present law, will enjoy enormous concessions with respect to their capital gains. Moreover, the retention of the nominally consistent provisions as to losses again lacks justification in terms of any fundamental considerations.

Congress may be congratulated for not adopting the proposed exemption of gains (and denial of deduction for losses) on property held over fifteen years. In the *Report* the supporting argument on this point is weak if not spurious and, at best, is rested on considerations of highly temporary significance. A fair apology might have been made, on the grounds that exemption is established by death of the owner in any event. But one raises here a problem of major importance.

The realization criterion is not only indispensable to a feasible income-tax system but relatively unobjectionable in principle where it results only in postponement of assessment, or in cancellation of earlier "paper profits" against subsequent paper losses. There are, however, almost unlimited opportunities for avoidance of tax where property passes, otherwise than by sale, out of the hands of the person in whose possession it has appreciated. Here one faces the question of what should be done as to personal income tax with respect to property transferred by gift, inheritance, and bequest.

Until 1921 no provision against such avoidance of tax was made in the American law. Gain or loss on property acquired by gift, inheritance, or bequest was calculated, in the case of beneficiaries, on the basis of the value of the property when acquired by them. Thus a person, transferring property to his children, could avoid not only estate and inheritance taxes but also income taxation with respect to any appreciation of the property in question. The 1921 Act and subsequent legislation has sought to prevent avoidance in the case of gifts *inter vivos*, but even here the achievement is not impressive.

The first legislation in this direction provided that gain or loss from the sale of property acquired by gift should be calculated on the same basis as if the sale had been made by the donor—i.e., generally, on the basis of cost to the donor. With respect to appreciated property, this arrangement would have merit under a strictly proportional tax and some merit from the viewpoint of the treasury in any event; but it represents not prevention of avoidance but only a sort of special tax upon it. After all, the tax is assessed against the donee, though it finds support in no considerations of equity as among donees or as between donees and other persons. Moreover, even on the revenue criterion, the treasury is but partly protected, for the gain will ordinarily be subject to lower rates in the hands of donees than in the hands of donors. While even such a crude device involved improvement over previous arrangements, one sees here again the folly of building an income tax around *ad rem* conceptions.

If the provisions with respect to gains are crude, the corresponding provisions as to losses were simply preposterous. What apology can possibly be offered for this blind pursuit of a nominal consistency? Why should individuals pay smaller income taxes merely because property which they acquired by gift had depreciated in the hands of the donor? Fortunately, the anomaly here has been removed from the law. The Revenue Act of 1934 provides (sec. 113) that "the basis shall be the same as it would be in the hands of the donor. . . . , except that for the purpose of determining loss the basis shall be the basis so determined *or* the fair market value of the property at the time of gift, whichever is lower."

There remains the question of why donees should be allowed any deductions whatever with respect to property acquired by gift. And the question invites a perhaps rather pointed comment: the present provisions as to the calculation of gain and loss on property acquired by gift would be entirely consistent with, and do not make sense without, provisions for the taxation of gifts themselves as income to the beneficiaries. If a wise visitor from Mars were to read sections 113 and 117 of our federal revenue act, he would surely infer that gifts were taxable as income.

If we have struggled rather unsuccessfully with problems of the realization criterion in the case of property transferred by gift, we have not even struggled in the case of transfers by inheritance and bequest. Thus we have a law which offers remarkable opportunities for people to reduce their personal tax by "realizing" on all properties which have depreciated and by leaving for sale by their beneficiaries all investments which have proved especially fortunate. Here one finds, in a sense, the most serious single fault in our income-tax system;

for, if this fault were corrected, many others would loom less large than they do now.[6]

The extension to property transferred through probate of the present rules with respect to gifts, while preferable to the continuance of present arrangements, could not be proposed with satisfaction or enthusiasm. There is no good reason for taxing the beneficiary, except as a revenue offset; the practice is cumbersome administratively; and the offset might seldom be realized in any event, for beneficiaries would certainly be least inclined to liquidate or shift investments on which the accumulated taxable gain was greatest. Moreover, as in the case of gifts, the gain would ordinarily be taxable in lower brackets in the hands of the beneficiary.

The appropriate solution would appear to be that of taxing all estates under the income tax just as though all property in the estate were disposed of at the fair market value as of the date of transfer to the beneficiary. The reconciliation which the realization criterion postpones must be effected some time, if wholesale avoidance is to be prevented; and many considerations, especially the fact that property must be appraised for probate and/or for estate and inheritance taxation in any event, would argue for reconciliation at the owner's death. Indeed, this would seem to be about the only sound and feasible method for effectively closing one of the major loopholes in our personal tax.

A strong case can also be made for altering the pro-

[6] The evasion with respect to undistributed corporate earnings especially. See below, chap. ix.

visions with respect to property transferred by gift to make them consistent with the above proposal. Every transfer of property by gift should be treated as a realization, at the fair market value as of the date of transfer, by the donor.[7] In the absence of such rules, appreciating property (especially stock of corporations reinvesting a large part of their earnings) might be transferred by gift from generation to generation so that the appreciation would never become taxable as income. The procedure, moreover, would be extremely convenient, since market value at the time of transfer must be determined in any event, for the calculation of losses in the hands of donees, for gift tax, and under the eminently desirable provision for the taxation of gifts as income to donees. The rule, if adopted, should

[7] In New York State the controller undertook (*Controller's Regulations*, Art. 91) to treat gifts as realizations to the donor, with respect to the state income tax of 1919. The New York Supreme Court, however, refused to sanction the controller's interpretation of the law (*Wilson* v. *Wendell*, 188 N.Y. Supp. 273–74; *Brewster* v. *Wendell*, 188 N.Y. Supp. 510–14).

The section of the statute prescribing the basis for calculating gain or loss reads as follows: "For the purpose of ascertaining the gain derived or loss sustained from the sale or other disposition of property . . . . the basis shall be . . . . " (*Laws of 1919*, c. 627, Art. 16, sec. 351). Interpreting the phrase "or other disposition of property" to include transfers by gift, the controller ruled that "gifts, whether charitable contributions or otherwise, constitute a disposition of property which may result in a profit or loss to be measured by the difference between the cost (or the value on January 1, 1919, if acquired prior thereto) and the value at the date of gift" (*Regulations*, Art. 91 [quoted, 188 N.Y. Supp. 513]). The opinions of the court, in both of the cases above, raise some question as to whether the procedure in question would be appropriate under a personal income tax; but the decisions are rested merely on the assertion that the *Controller's Regulations* involved an improper construction of the statute: "To give it the construction asserted by the comptroller is to extend the provisions of the act by implication 'beyond the import of the language used' . . . ." (188 N.Y. Supp. 514).

also be applicable even to gifts which are deductible (within the 15 per cent limitation) in the calculation of taxable income—e.g., to gifts of property for charitable purposes.

It may be useful, in summary, to bring together the proposals made above:

1. All gifts, inheritances, and bequests should be treated as income of the recipients for the year in which received.

2. Every transfer of property by gift, inheritance or bequest should be treated as a realization, at the estimated fair market value, by the donor or by the deceased owner's estate.

3. Gains and losses from the sale of property acquired by gift, inheritance, or bequest should be calculated on the basis of fair market value at the time of transfer (as estimated for purposes of two provisions above).

The adoption of these proposals would enable us to displace a set of crude, inadequate, stopgap expedients by an elegant, coherent set of rules; it would purge our great personal tax of a large accumulation of *ad rem* anomalies; and it would leave no major loophole through which gains might permanently escape inclusion in taxable income. Sometime it may become feasible to place even less reliance on the realization criterion. Perhaps taxpayers might be required decennially to report their taxable incomes as though all property were disposed of at estimated fair market values as of that year. Ultimately, this reconciliation might be made annually, and the income tax supplemented by a moderate, mildly progressive levy on persons according to net worth, as reflected in reported inventories of all assets and obligations. For the moment, however, it is imperative that we eliminate from the income-tax system both the many anomalous *ad rem* elements and the opportunities for wholesale evasion which are attributable to *uncritical* reliance on the realization criterion. A solid structure of income-tax legislation must ultimately reach all gains in the hands of the person to whom they accrue (or in the hands of his estate), and it must be such as to require accounting under the income tax for all acquisitions and transfers of property.

ADDENDUM

There remains the possibility, under the arrangements here proposed, of postponing tax payments and thus of retaining the use of funds which, under an income-tax procedure involving annual reappraisal of investment assets, would be payable to the government at earlier dates. Enjoying large gains, realizable but unrealized, one could in effect borrow from the treasury without interest, sometimes for many years. While this possibility indicates a significant difference between the "ideal" methods of calculating taxable income and the modified realization procedure, there would seem to be no serious inequities involved in adherence to the methods which practical considerations so strongly dictate. Persons obtaining large unrealized profits in their youth might be advantaged somewhat, as against those whose financial good fortune came later in life. On the other hand, there is much to be said for arrangements which permit persons, as investors in operating companies (if not in holding companies or investment trusts), to reinvest freely, without annual taxation of their paper profits, provided the full amount of their gains will ultimately be subject to tax. (A very convincing case, where the considerations in question were actually decisive against an otherwise attractive and commendable undertaking, has recently come to the author's attention.) Moreover, the treasury is protected in most cases against abuse of the postponement opportunities, for wholesale postponement would ordinarily subject the income, when realized, to much higher surtax rates. What a man may gain by postponing realization will ordinarily be offset, or more than offset, under progressive rates, by the piling-up of taxable income in his later years or in the hands of his estate. If this offset or inhibition is not effective in the case of persons continuously subject to the topmost surtax rates, the treasury eventually will get the greater part (now 79 per cent) of what the taxpayer saves or gains by postponing payment anyway.

It is sometimes argued that undesirable avoidance arises where large, unrealized gains are later offset by losses. This contention suggests undue preoccupation with the "maximum-revenue" criterion and implies that even more discrimination against persons of widely fluctuating incomes is desirable. In the author's opinion, it is a great merit of the modified realization procedure that it mitigates the penalty of progression upon irregularity and enables the taxpayer to level out fluctuations in his annual taxable income. Full application of accrual procedures, with annual revaluation of investment assets, on the other hand, would serve greatly to increase the fluctuations and, thus, would call for generous and complicated devices of averaging—or would make the tax much more inequitable if such devices were not introduced.

CHAPTER VIII

TAX-EXEMPT SECURITIES

ANY exemption of receipts by kind is clearly incompatible with the essential rationale of income taxes. The base of such taxes is properly a measure of the relative prosperity of individuals, and no data relevant to such measurement can be disregarded or excluded without distortion of the relative levies upon persons. We have noted, as a conspicuous fault of American legislation, the disregard of the net receipts from real property used by its owner for consumption purposes and, as a fault common to levies both here and abroad, the partial or complete exclusion of capital gains and losses. The neglect of gratuitous receipts is likewise anomalous and unfortunate. Most flagrant and least pardonable of all such errors of omission, however, is the exemption of the interest and salary payments of governmental bodies. The other omissions find some explanation, if only in terms of strange misconceptions; the relevant questions of policy are still controversial, whether they should be or not. But hardly anyone would pretend to justify the deliberate exemption of interest on governmental obligations; for any government which does this is violating its responsibility for levying personal taxes equitably.

Interest on the obligations of our states and their political subdivisions is entirely exempt from federal income tax, by statute (sec. 22b [4]), and is generally held to be exempt on constitutional grounds.[1] Amounts received as compensation for services rendered to such governmental units by their officials and regular employes are likewise exempt.[2] Other similar exemptions are a matter of deliberate action by Congress, or by the treasury under discretionary powers granted by Congress to the secretary. One small issue of Liberty Bonds carried complete exemption; other issues carried strange partial exemptions of a varied and complicated nature. Secretary Mellon (after urging amendment to abolish all exemptions) inaugurated a policy of issuing short-term obligations with full exemption (to enable the treasury to compete with the states and municipalities!). This policy has bloomed in fuller ugliness under Mr. Morgenthau, whose advisors and assistants evidently have felt that any means was justified in the flotation of short-term issues at spectacularly low rates of yield. Supreme among the extant fiscal monstrosities, however, is the grant of income-tax exemptions with respect to the bonds of federal corporations like the land banks,

[1] Some authorities (Corwin, notably) have questioned this view. The position commonly imputed to the Court certainly has little to commend it on logical grounds; but, after tacit acceptance for many years, it may now be regarded as properly amenable to change by the straightforward procedure of constitutional amendment—however inadequate the reasoning behind the position. See below, pp. 202 ff.

[2] This exemption, unlike that of interest, is a matter of administrative ruling, not of statute—although the Act of 1926 (sec. 1211) excluded such compensation under prior acts. The treasury has conferred the administrative exemption only with respect to compensation for services rendered in connection with the exercise of an essential governmental function (a nice distinction!), thus leaving the salary payments of municipal utilities subject to tax. The definition of "officer or employee" also limits the exemption quite narrowly. See *Regulations 86*, pp. 212–13.

and joint-stock land banks. One might compile an engaging list of fiscal vagaries which owe their existence to that strange stigma which attaches to straightforward and explicit subsidies (in a nation where indirect tariff subsidies are innumerable and transparent); and this one might well head that list.

The exemption of salaries paid by our state and local governments is a minor (but thoroughly objectionable) kind of fault. The beneficiaries of this exemption will seldom have much other income, and government salaries rarely expose them to high rates of tax. A few people, to be sure, will be grossly undertaxed; but no important opportunities are created for deliberate evasion.

The exemption of the interest payments on an enormous amount of government bonds, on the other hand, is a flaw of major importance. It opens the way to deliberate avoidance on a grand scale; and it provides a method of avoidance which must give rise to serious inequities and to some diseconomies. The method is not available to persons whose large incomes are derived from salaries and fees. It is not easily accessible to persons, active in the control and management of enterprises, whose investments cannot be diversified without loss of the desired control over their firms. Indeed, this device of avoidance is entirely attractive only to the idle, passive holders of highly conservative investments. Thus the exemption not only undermines the program of progressive personal taxation but also introduces a large measure of differentiation in favor of those whose role in our economy is merely that of *rentiers*.

The exemption, of course, carries a price. With strictly proportional levies, the yield differential attributable to the exemption would probably reflect its full value to all purchasers. With progressive rates, however, a fully compensating yield differential is impossible, unless the exempt obligations are very scarce and are held entirely by persons paying the maximum rates of surtax. Even in these circumstances there will be unfortunate windfalls of gain or loss whenever the rates of tax are changed in a manner which the market has not anticipated fully. Thus, the holders of our state and local obligations were greatly benefited by the rapid development of our federal income tax—while the debtor agencies gained only with respect to their new borrowings.[3]

· Actually, tax-exempt securities are abundant; and they are not held even mainly by persons subject to the highest surtaxes. The yield differential reflects the value of exemption only to the so-called middle-income groups —or to persons of large income for whom investment in "tax exempts" involves large disadvantages or "disutilities." Most taxpayers cannot afford the exemption at all; some would only break even; but the *rentier* of great wealth finds here a tremendous bargain. Here, at

---

[3] It is an interesting anomaly that, despite the Sixteenth Amendment, our federal government, in order to impose or increase its personal taxes, must contribute heavily toward the costs of state and local borrowing. The powers reserved to the states, of course, must not be impaired. It seems a weird kind of rhetorical legerdemain, however, which finds in this principle both a prohibition against the equitable imposition of personal taxes and the requirement of large and curious subsidies to the states as payment for the limited exercise of a prerogative which has been granted to the federal government specifically and unreservedly.

last, is a "commodity" with respect to which the traditional and naïve conception of "consumer surplus" has clear meaning and significance. The value of additional increments of exemption to him will show continued (if not continuous) decline; but the value of the early increments remains precisely the same, however many increments are added; and a summation of the incremental values measures properly the value of his "stock." And it is precisely this "consumer surplus" which reflects the folly of the exemption.

Professor Hardy, after interesting analysis of a mass of data, came to the conclusion that the practice of exemption actually worked out profitably, for all our taxing and borrowing agencies together, up to 1924.[4] The inadequacies of his method for determining the yield differential, to be sure, all eased the way to this startling conclusion; but a more serious criticism is in order. Hardy appears to offer his statistical work as demonstrating that tax exemption, as a serious problem, is merely a creature of uninformed minds. The author never says this, to be sure; but the tone of the book is such that failure to disavow the implication is equivalent to assertion of the position. Let us concede that all governmental units together were coming out about even with respect to the tax-exempt securities. (In view of the bias in his methods, this is a generously small

---

[4] C. O. Hardy, *Tax Exempt Securities and the Surtax* (New York, 1926), esp. chap. iv. The only evident flaw in his statistical analysis (but a very serious one) lies in his obviously biased method for calculating the yield differential. For other calculations, similar in their methods and in their results, see Hinrichs, "The Cost of Tax Exempt Securities," *Political Science Quarterly*, XLI (1926), 271–80.

amendment of Hardy's actual results.) What now would be the significance of such a fact for the question of policy?

The essential point here has to do with the "maximum-revenue criterion." Its shortcomings, as a guide for policy in personal taxation, have been noted in previous chapters; and they are not less great in this instance than in others. The problem of tax-exempt securities is perhaps largely illusory, *unless* one happens to be interested in the income tax as a means for reaching persons equitably and progressively; but from that viewpoint it is terribly real.[5]

The government will not lose heavily in the case of all large taxpayers. Many of them will find it impossible, unprofitable, or unattractive to convert their incomes into a tax-exempt form. An individual may be unwilling to abandon control of enterprises which have been largely his own; he may be able to obtain a much larger income by combining his investments with active participation in management; or he may greatly prefer the active business role which concentration of his investment permits, even with small or negligible remuneration for his services. But the avoidance of revenue losses in the case of such persons means a most inequi-

[5] Hardy conceded this point as soon as it was raised against his book, by the present writer and by others previously. Our criticism is directed against a position which his book implies, not against one which he actually holds. Moreover, the book itself, in spite of minor faults which we have noted, was an important and substantial contribution. It was abundantly informing; it exposed clearly the arrant sophistries of Mr. Mellon; and it discredited the statistical extravagances of writers like Seligman, whose sound enthusiasm for abolition of the exemptions had led them into unsound argument, careless assertions, and essentially irrelevant discussion.

table distribution of tax burdens as between them and others of similar income circumstances. Broadly speaking, it means gross differentiation within the upper brackets in favor of coupon clippers and against those actively engaged in business enterprise—which hardly commends the arrangement!

In any case, there will certainly be a heavy net loss with respect to persons of great wealth; the governments can only lose in the case of persons who acquire the securities for the exemption. Where, then, could there be gains to offset this loss? The answer must lie in a highly inelastic demand for exempt securities on the part of other purchasers; and these other purchasers, obviously, are corporations and individuals not subject to high surtax rates. The inelasticity of their demand may be attributed (*a*) to the nature and traditions of certain businesses and to legal requirements regarding the investments of financial corporations and (*b*) to the disposition of many thrifty persons to buy governmental obligations almost regardless of yield. The lower yields resulting from the valuable exemption can have but limited effect on the portfolios of life insurance companies, of savings banks, and of ordinary people who distrust, as regards other investments, both their own judgment and the kind of advice available to them.

Thus, if governments did break even on the exemption practice, they could do so only by forcing a lower rate of return upon intramarginal buyers of government bonds—i.e., only if those who purchase for the exemption force down the yields without altering greatly the amount of exempt securities held by persons and institutions to whom the exemption has little or no value. Those who purchase for the exemption may greatly reduce their tax payments; but their purchases will permit the marketing of new issues at lower rates of yield. Those who lose by the arrangement are the conservative investors of small means and the financial institutions which serve largely the middle- and lower-income groups. The exemption practice is thus doubly regressive in its burden: it compels recourse to excises for revenues which would otherwise have come from persons of large means and, for people of small means, it lowers the return on their investments and increases the costs of insurance and annuities.

The whole policy of exemption works out like a subsidy, distributed in the form of relief from surtaxes and financed by levies upon small savers. So, one may well reverse Hardy's implication and assert that the results of the policy would probably be less objectionable, on any reasonable welfare criteria, if it showed a heavy fiscal loss than if no loss or a gain were involved. Heavy loss would be indicative of a more uniform scaling-down of the burdens on persons of large income; while the absence of loss implies gross discrimination among such persons and a heavy regression burden on other groups as well.

The policy may also be interpreted as one of offering governmental obligations to different persons on widely different terms—as a strange sort of class-price policy in the sale of securities. If you are subject to the highest rates of surtax, you are offered, in effect, a return of about 12 per cent on your investments in state and local obligations; if your income does not expose you to federal income tax, you are offered about 3 per cent. One hardly need ask whether it would be desirable or politically possible to do openly and straightforwardly what is accomplished here by indirection—and by deliberate action as well as by errors of omission.

And other counts may be added to the indictment. The exemption, along with other faults of the law, enables us, and our political representatives especially, to enjoy all the moral satisfaction of imposing radical and drastic levies on great wealth without actually doing so. The discrimination against those who obtain large incomes from salaries, or by combining their investments with active participation in business, is deplorable, both on economic and on ethical grounds. The indirect subsidizing of the states and their subdivisions is thoroughly bad not in itself but because the subsidy is allocated in proportion to borrowing. Finally, the effects on our whole investment situation are exceedingly unfortunate. Those who should absorb the more speculative issues are forced into a kind of investment which should largely be reserved for those whose total investments are too small to permit real diversification or to support thorough investment analysis. Those who should buy nothing else are turned away from government bonds by their scarcity and low yield; and persons who, with their statisticians and professional analysts, should arbitrate the direction of new and speculative undertaking can now be attracted away from exempt investments only by prospects of fabulous yields. On all these scores, exemption does things which would seem preposterous if done straightforwardly.

Our federal law has sought to avoid some anomalies by partial prohibition of the deduction of interest "on indebtedness incurred or continued to purchase or carry" tax-exempt securities (sec. 23*b*). The rationale of this provision is obvious enough. Suppose that a maximum rate of 75 per cent is levied with respect to personal income in excess of $10,000,000; and take the case of a person whose taxable income is consistently in excess of that amount. This individual borrows, let us say, $10,000,000 at 4 per cent, posting gilt-edge securities as collateral, and uses the proceeds of the loan to purchase 3 per cent municipal bonds at par. On the face of it, he loses $100,000 annually by such an operation; but the interest deduction would reduce his taxable income by $400,000 and reduce his tax payment by $300,000 annually. The operation thus would show a net profit of $200,000 after taxes.

While the law clearly prohibits this device of evasion, the prohibition is entirely ineffective. Congress may rest comfortable in the notion that it has dealt with the problem; actually, it has only laid down an ambiguous and unenforceable rule; for application of the rule requires determination of purpose or intention. How may the treasury or the courts determine whether particular debts are incurred or continued for the purpose of purchasing or carrying particular securities? Here again is the naïve notion that particular items on the right-hand side of a balance sheet are represented by particular items on the left-hand side. Actually, the interest deduction is denied only in the case of collateral loans which are secured by the deposit of tax-exempt securities.[6] Thus, this device of avoidance is really prohibited only in the case of persons unable to provide other good collateral and unable to borrow without collateral— i.e., only in the case of persons of small means!

Secretary Mellon once proposed a revision of this section which would have made the prohibition what it now only seems to be. His excellent suggestion was that taxpayers be permitted to deduct as interest only the amount by which their interest expense exceeded their tax-exempt income.[7] Acting on this suggestion, Congress might have rescued section 23b from absurdity; but the appropriate legislation was not forthcoming. There were doubtless many misgivings on constitutional grounds. However, while the prohibition ought to be either made effective or repealed outright, there is clearly no important mitigation of the tax-exemption difficulty to be found along these lines. Moreover, Mr. Mellon's scheme is less attractive when one examines it more closely.

There is little reason why anyone should resort to these borrowing tricks, unless the costs involved in outright transfer of one's investments are unusually high. Why should anyone borrow to purchase "tax exempts"

[6] Where tax-exempt securities represent only part of the collateral, only a proportionate part of the interest on the loan is nondeductible. See Montgomery, *Federal Income Tax Handbook, 1936–37*, p. 497.

[7] Letter from the Secretary of the Treasury to the acting chairman of the Committee on Ways and Means, November 10, 1923. Reprinted in Mellon, *Taxation: The People's Business* (New York, 1924), Appen. A (see pp. 183–84).

unless all his investments promise to yield a higher rate of interest than that at which he can borrow? Looking at the matter in this light, one sees that the proposed legislation would not limit appreciably the opportunities for evasion, among persons subject to high rates, except in the case of those actively engaged in business. The limitation would be quite innocuous for persons whose property is largely in conservative and diversified investments and whose role in business is essentially passive. On the other hand, it would close this avenue of avoidance for persons unwilling to adopt that role and unable to diversify their commitments without undue loss of managerial control. On grounds of fairness among persons of large income, it may thus be argued that such backhanded and partial nullification of the exemptions might do more harm than good. If we are to offer large opportunities for evasion of high surtaxes, these opportunities should not be made available to people of similar incomes on more unequal and more unreasonably different terms. But, to repeat, the existing rule should either be implemented or repealed. The law is now overcrowded with empty, verbal solutions of totally unsolved problems.

There can be no satisfactory solution apart from the complete removal of the specific exemptions. An appropriate amendment to the Constitution has repeatedly been recommended to Congress in presidential messages. One may regret the necessity of amendment; and one may feel that it would be unwise now (1936) for intelligent conservatives to recommend even the most desirable constitutional changes; but the considerations in question are less important in a case like this one, where the question of policy is not controversial. The question of policy was settled by the adoption of the Sixteenth Amendment. There is now no real dispute as to whether the federal government should levy a tax upon persons according to their respective income circumstances. The exemption situation simply prohibits the equitable imposition of such a tax—prohibits indeed any adequate realization of the purposes implicit in the Sixteenth Amendment. Whether the blame lies with those who drafted the amendment or with the Court (or with the treasury and its legal counsel) is now perhaps an academic question.

The important problem now is that of inducing Congress to propose, and the states to ratify, an amendment which can have no intelligent opposition. As things stand, the borrowing states and their subdivisions do enjoy a substantial federal subsidy; and some opposition must arise against any measure which would both make our surtaxes more effective and increase the direct costs of state and local borrowing. The long-continued and deliberate inaction of Congress suggests the necessity of wise political maneuvering; and the situation admits of good measures for overcoming opposition based on the vested interests in the borrowing subsidy. At worst, the federal government might undertake, for a considerable period, to subsidize every state to the extent of, say, 1 per cent annually of its new bond issues (including those of its subdivisions). At best, Congress and the administration might promise a generous sharing of federal income-tax revenues with the states, as soon as the amendment was ratified. A division of revenues on the basis of collections seems eminently desirable in itself (see below, chap. x); and it might wisely be held out as an inducement for the proposal and ratification of an amendment abolishing all the exemptions now seemingly required by the Constitution and the Court.

ADDENDUM

Most discussion presupposes that the appropriate amendment would affect only future issues of the states and their subdivisions. The interest on "tax exempts" previously outstanding would presumably remain exempt until they were retired or refunded; and most reformers are reconciled to the gradual disappearance of exempt interest which would thus be involved. Haste may be foolish in such matters; but it may be interesting to consider a scheme whereby immediate abolition of all exemptions would be accompanied by federal payment to holders of securities previously exempt of enough additional interest (say, 1 per cent at most) to prevent any decline in the value of such property on account of the removal of the exemption. The legal possibilities of such a scheme, and the proper tricks in the phrasing of the amendment, are for lawyers to determine. To the layman, however, it would appear to provide adequately for every legitimate vested interest; and it would prevent the large windfalls of gain which would otherwise accrue to the holders of exempt securities of distant maturity.

Incidentally, if we are to have an amendment to eliminate specific exemptions under the income tax, it would certainly be appropriate to append a sentence or paragraph specifically granting to Congress the broadest powers as regards definition of the tax base. If the ruling interpretation of the Sixteenth Amendment is to follow the reasoning (if one may call it that) of *Eisner* v. *Macomber* (the stock-dividend case), every substantial change in the prescribed rules for calculating taxable income must be made with, at the least, grave uncertainties as to what the Supreme Court might decide about its constitutionality. Unless the Court henceforth displays a measure of insight which it has never revealed to date, the impossible question of what is income and what is not income (see chaps. ii and iii above) will remain with us as a perpetual legal issue. The only appropriate limitation upon legislative powers in this matter would confer upon the Court the power to invalidate legislation which operated in a grossly inequitable manner as among persons, i.e., which discriminated grossly and arbitrarily between and among persons of substantially similar circumstances.

CHAPTER IX

UNDISTRIBUTED CORPORATE EARNINGS

WHILE the most serious structural faults of our federal income tax (and of foreign taxes especially) have to do with capital gains and capital losses, the practical difficulties here are attributable mainly to the corporate entity and the corporate fiction. Only through corporations is it possible for individuals easily and systematically to avoid income tax with respect to their savings or to convert their incomes into a partially taxable (or exempt) capital-gain form. In a different kind of treatise these problems of personal taxation which arise out of the peculiar legal status of the corporation might properly be made the subject of a long chapter or section. Here, however, they must be dealt with briefly, for systematic discussion would be grossly repetitious. The problems in question are simply not problems at all under the scheme of levy defined by the proposals of previous chapters (esp. chap. vii). If every disposition of property were made the occasion for a gain-or-loss calculation to a seller, a donor, or an estate, the corporation would simply cease to be means for successful avoidance of personal taxes. So, in this chapter, we shall undertake merely to note some of the devices which have been invoked to deal with these problems in the past and to strengthen the case for measures which we have proposed by indicating the limitations of other possible schemes.

Partial and nominal prohibitions against the evasion practices in question have long been part of English and American law. There is the familiar section 102 (formerly sec. 220) of our federal income tax and the similar provisions of the English statutes. Such legislation, however, only means that the problem has been formally recognized. It represents merely a verbal concession to protests against inequity. Our section 102 (and its counterparts in earlier statutes) has never been, and could never be, really enforced. Its application requires determination of intention or purpose; and, if the administrative rulings mean anything at all, only stupidity could expose corporations to its penalties. Accumulation of earnings must be in excess of "the reasonable needs of the business"; so long as funds are employed for any ordinary purpose, accumulation evidently is not "unreasonable." A company may expand plant, buy out competitors, expand its advertising, retire its bonds or other obligations, or even repurchase its preferred stock; indeed, it apparently may accumulate earnings without any penalty, so long as it does not confess, in its balance sheet, that it has more funds than it can use advantageously.

The English prohibitions explicitly relate to "family corporations" (companies whose stock is very closely held); and earlier administrative rulings practically served to confine the application of (now) section 102 to such cases. Some teeth have recently been put into the American law by the enactment of the special surtax on personal holding companies (sec. 351). This measure, obviously designed to penalize practices which had been widely publicized in cases like that of Mr. Andrew Mellon, and carrying higher rates than the penalties of section 102, makes that section even more useless than it was before. As *ad hoc* legislation, it has merit; but no special tax, restricted to holding companies and to cases where half of the outstanding stock is owned by not more than five persons, can do more than require recourse to slightly different and perhaps, at the moment, less convenient devices of avoidance. It affords no protection whatever against avoidance through large investment trusts organized to provide the means of tax-free accumulation of income to a numerous clientele, or against avoidance through family corporations not in the nature of holding companies (as defined by sec. 351).

Section 102 might possibly be interpreted to cover these cases. But this legislation, while mandatory in form, actually serves only to confer broad powers on the administrative authority (and awful responsibilities on the courts). The tests of its applicability are hopelessly vague; and the offense in question is defined in utterly ambiguous terms of degree. Thus, it cannot really be called a tax; and its levies are far too moderate to function effectively as fines or penalties. Not only is section 102 vague and indefinite and section 351 unduly limited in scope but they both have all the inevitable faults of *ad rem* expedients in a system of personal taxation. No taxes on corporations can correct inequities in relative personal levies, unless they are drastic enough simply to prohibit the corporation practices which involve personal evasion; and prohibitory levies involve disturbing changes in corporation law which, while possibly desirable in other grounds, ought not to be guided merely by income-tax considerations. Moreover, in the cases before us, the maximum rates imposed are 25 per cent (35 per cent for companies not subject to the undistributed earnings tax) under section 102, and 48 per cent under section 351; while the rate of personal tax avoided by shareholders may be as high as 79 per cent!

The same criticism applies to our most recent undertaking in the prevention of surtax avoidance, namely, the new tax on undistributed corporate earnings (sec. 14). This legislation has been most unintelligently and unreasonably condemned in many circles; but, while superior perhaps to any other scheme which might have been sponsored successfully at the time, it cannot be regarded as a solution of the problem with which it deals. Failing or pending adoption of the measures proposed in chapter vii above, it deserves to be continued, with gradual increase in its rates. Like section 351, however, it is a crude *ad rem* gadget; and like the exemption of interest on state and local obligations, it will serve, by imposing specific penalties on certain practices, to confine the avoidance opportunities to persons of rather large means. Even 27 per cent is a moderate charge for the privilege of avoiding a rate of 79 per cent. Thus, about all we can hope to accomplish through legislative tricks of this sort is a discouragement of evasion practices on the part of ordinary corporations with numerous shareholders not subject to high rates of surtax—i.e., on the part of corporations not organized specifically for evasion purposes and not able to manage their affairs primarily with regard for the interests of very wealthy shareholders. Existing devices only invite a tremendous development of investment trusts[1] designed to provide for large taxpayers the blessings of sections 117 and 113a (5).[2]

Another possible scheme for dealing with the problem of undistributed corporate earnings is that of treating all corporations simply as partnerships for purposes of personal taxation. The legal difficulties which this procedure might involve need not concern us here. Corporations may now elect to be so treated, to escape the levies of section 102 or section 351. This procedure is

[1] The 1936 Act does introduce an additional penalty in such cases. Eighty-five per cent of the dividends received by a corporation (formerly 100 per cent) are exempt from the corporation normal tax. This exemption has now been removed in the case of "mutual investment companies," as defined in sec. 48e; but such companies, in lieu of the credit for dividends received, are granted a credit of 100 per cent with respect to dividends paid (sec. 13a).

The detailed provisions of sec. 48e are interesting and mainly admirable. They might well be followed closely in the reform of corporation law along lines which the author has elsewhere suggested (A Positive Program for Laissez Faire [Chicago, 1934], pp. 19–20). However, one may question the wisdom of subsec. (1)(E), which denies special treatment to the investment trust unless "its shareholders are, upon reasonable notice, entitled to redemption of their stock for their proportionate interest in the corporation's properties, or the cash equivalent thereof less a discount not in excess of 3 per centum thereof." This subsection appears to discriminate arbitrarily and unreasonably against companies which merit no such treatment; and it encourages a form of contract which is not essential to sound investment-trust organization and which, indeed, is likely to prove highly undesirable.

[2] The undistributed earnings tax has been criticized for its failure to provide exemptions for corporations which, by virtue of accumulated deficits, are unable under state law to pay out dividends from current earnings. On the other hand, one may well argue that the credits now permitted with respect to "contracts restricting payment of dividends" are inappropriate; for any reinvestment, voluntary or obligatory, involves avoidance of personal income taxes. The credits denied (by omission) are not less reasonable perhaps

required by the corresponding provisions of the English law. Should it not be employed for all corporations?

That it would involve serious administrative difficulties is apparent immediately. The worst of these have to do with the allocating of undistributed earnings among different classes of owners. If all corporations were thoroughly solvent, and if their security issues were uniformly restricted to three or four standard contract forms, the task would not be altogether forbidding. Difficulties of principle would still arise; but they probably could be dealt with adequately by rule-of-thumb devices. On the other hand, where companies have a great variety of contracts with their investors, and where some classes of securities represent no clear equity at all, apportionment is almost out of the question. The names of securities tell one almost nothing;[3] and the

---

than the ones granted; but both, to say the least, are questionable. If we must be satisfied merely with *ad rem* charges for surtax avoidance, should we permit persons to escape even these indirect charges by utilizing the charters of companies which happen to have had financial misfortunes in the past, or happen to have entered into dividend-limiting contracts with their creditors? To withhold the credits in question will work some hardships; to grant them would be to invite deliberate (as well as fortuitous) evasion. That a dilemma of this kind should arise merely testifies to the crudity and inadequacy of the whole scheme.

Likewise questionable is the exemption of particular corporations according to the kind of business in which they are engaged—of the banks and insurance companies especially. (They are also exempt under sec. 351.) Incidentally, many people must now (1936) be investigating the possibilities of using foreign incorporation for purposes of surtax avoidance.

[3] Here one finds a serious fault in the distinction (abandoned in the Revenue Act of 1936) between preferred-stock dividends (exempt) and bond interest (taxable) for purposes of personal normal tax. Certainly the corporation income tax affects equities more adversely in the case of many bondholders than in the case of the owners of gilt-edge preferred stocks.

specific terms of investment contracts have clear meaning only for the normal (?) case of prosperous, conservatively financed enterprises.

Good apportionment of corporate earnings would require thorough investigation of every individual company and careful appraisal of its earnings prospects. One should know the specific terms of all outstanding contracts, the various rights and options attaching to different kinds of shares, and the financial condition and outlook of the enterprise as well. If it were possible to locate a single class of truly residual claimants, the task would not be so hard. But what should be done with badly financed concerns or with those unable ordinarily to distribute anything to one or more classes of investors? Suppose that, in a particular case, interest has been paid on mortgage bonds unfailingly, on debentures with occasional omissions, on income bonds usually; that preferred dividends have been paid infrequently; and that nothing has ever been paid on the common stock. In the fiscal year just closed, earnings have for the first time been large, and, no dividend being declared on the common stock, a substantial reduction has been made in the accumulated deficit. Following publication of the financial statements, the market values of the securities increase as follows: common stock, from $1 to $5; preferred shares, from $20 to $50; income bonds, from $40 to $80; debentures, from $75 to $90; and mortgage bonds, from $90 to $95. How shall the undivided profits be allocated among the various equities?

Such difficult cases might be avoided by permitting accumulation of small surpluses without apportionment;

but this concession has even more serious disadvantages here than in the undistributed earnings tax. It involves taking names too seriously and would work properly only if the holdings and personnel of shareholders never changed at all (i.e., only in Mr. Keynes's ideal economy where all private investment commitments were irreversible). Should a group of persons, buying up at nominal prices the stock of companies whose books show no stockholder equity, be permitted to escape personal tax on an amount of earnings equal to the par value of their stock? What should be done where reinvestment serves mainly to improve the uncertain position of creditors or to increase the value of outstanding options to purchase treasury stock? Such questions suggest no satisfactory answers. It should be evident, however, that any simple exemption from apportionment would work out badly as regards the relative taxation of persons and that, without such exemptions, the scheme is forbidding administratively.

Even for highly solvent firms, the apportionment of earnings would be inordinately complicated where an elaborate variety of arrangements prevailed as to different kinds of stock. Fixed and residual claimants can be distinguished only in terms of probabilities and in the light of particular circumstances. The reinvestment of earnings will usually increase the value of preference shares, in varying degree depending upon the normal margin and fluctuations of earnings and upon the nature of conversion options, where they exist. All these difficulties notwithstanding, the apportionment scheme might become feasible (if not desirable) if drastic changes, desirable on other grounds,[4] were made in our laws defining and limiting corporate powers. If incorporated enterprises were required to maintain large residual equities, and were permitted only a small number of security contracts in rigidly prescribed forms, then earnings might easily be allocated on a per share basis for purposes of personal tax. But income-tax schemes, dependent for their successful operation on ideal solutions of problems in other areas of economic policy, do not merit very serious consideration.

Under the most favorable circumstances, moreover, the apportionment procedure would complicate considerably the calculation of gains and losses when securities were sold (or otherwise disposed of). Treating all corporations as partnerships would require that shareholders be granted the same kind of credits as those now provided for partners, by administrative ruling.[5] From capital gains as now calculated it would be necessary to subtract (and to capital losses, to add) the amount of the shareholder's interest in corporate earnings reinvested during the period in question. In other words, gain or loss at time of sale would have to be computed as follows: add dividends received to the proceeds of the sale and then subtract the sum of original cost of the stock plus the total of earnings reported with respect to the stock by the shareholder for personal tax. (Account would be taken, of course, only of dividends re-

[4] I.e., mainly on grounds which concern the monopoly problem. See the writer's *A Positive Program for Laissez Faire*, and also a short paper, "The Requisites of Free Competition," *American Economic Review Supplement*, March, 1936, pp. 68–76.

[5] See *Regulations 86*, sec. 113a (13)–2.

ceived and earnings reported during the period between the purchases and sales in question.) While the procedure would make it possible to leave dividends out of account ordinarily, they would have to be brought into the accounting whenever stock was sold (and, properly, whenever it was given away or transferred through probate).

If corporations were treated as partnerships, one might argue more plausibly for the ignoring of capital gains and losses for purposes of the personal tax.[6] But the case would still be very weak; for even ideal allocations of corporate income can afford only crude (and, properly, only tentative) presumptions as to personal income. Corporation balance sheets and income reports will reflect valuations different, and often widely different, from market values. A company's earning power may increase (or decrease) greatly and rapidly without much change in current earnings. This sort of change may arise from appreciation of real estate, from the growth of good-will, from secure establishment of dubious patent rights, from perfection of administrative organization, from solution of labor difficulties, or from discharge of dishonest officials; it may come from the suppression of formerly dangerous competition or from prospective economies in transportation expenses. Certainly such changes would have little effect on current earnings, as calculated for the corporation tax. For shareholders and for the markets, however, they have the same kind of significance as an increase of physical

[6] One of the grave practical dangers of the recent levy upon undistributed corporate earnings is that it may weaken greatly the resistance to this change.

capacity effected through the use of funds which might have been used for dividends. The shareholder's gains or losses obviously depend not merely on what the corporation earns during his participation as an owner but also upon the terms on which he acquires and disposes of his interest in the business. If apportionment is proper for purposes of tentative measurement of gains or losses, it would not eliminate the need for an ultimate and definitive reconciliation, on the occasion of sale, gift, or transfer at death.

These complications are avoided under the simple expedient of the undistributed earnings tax—and properly enough, since the purpose of this expedient is not that of effecting equitable personal taxation directly but merely that of discouraging through penalty certain practices which result in evasion of personal taxes. They are also avoided partially, and less properly, under sections 102 and 351. Corporations may escape the levies imposed by these two sections if their shareholders elect to be treated as partners. If this option is exercised, any subsequent distribution from earnings of the year in question (i.e., presumably, subsequent distributions in excess of subsequent earnings) are not taxable to the shareholders. But the exemption seems to apply even though the payment is made to persons other than the shareholders who actually reported as partners; and the shareholder who sells his stock presumably must calculate his taxable gain or loss without regard for the amount of undistributed earnings previously taxed to him.[7]

[7] It may be improper to discuss the detailed application of legislation which has never really been applied. If cases ever arose, like those we have

The scheme outlined in chapter vii above avoids all these complications and reveals none of the conspicuous limitations of other devices for preventing the evasion of personal tax with respect to undistributed earnings. It is a solution, not a temporary, stopgap expedient. It introduces no unfortunate *ad rem* elements into the system; and it would simply preclude avoidance of personal tax by the methods in question. It involves no real impairment of the existing system of procedure based on the realization criterion; and it calls for no modification of existing rules of law as to the corporate fiction. Not least of its merits, moreover, is that it would serve to minimize the arbitrary influence of taxation upon corporation finance and dividend policies.[8]

ADDENDUM

Let us now append a few unsophisticated remarks about relevant legal conceptions and judicial analysis.

The approved procedure, of course, is that of taxing shareholders with respect to dividends received and, very partially,

---

described above, the treasury might allow a reasonable credit to the seller, just as it has done, without specific authorization, in the case of partners (see *Regulations 86*, sec. 113a(13)–2); but if it did so, it would apparently be impossible under the law to withhold the credit from the buyer in case a distribution from the earnings in question were made to him.

[8] That the recent levy on undistributed earnings will have awful effects on this score is a notion which has been fabricated out of little information and less understanding and for no very noble purposes. The benefits will far outweigh any slightly untoward effects. To be sure, there is urgent need for drastic changes in our corporation law (see, for the writer's position, the references in n. 4, p. 193); and curious tax devices may incidentally yield some of the desirable effects which would follow from sound legislation of a more straightforward and fundamental character. However, reform pro-

with respect to gains derived from the sale of stock. Administrative rulings, and court decisions especially, imply the existence of a tangible something called "corporate income," which, by virtue of certain transactions between the company and its owners, can be transmuted into personal income. Lawyers find it comfortably obvious that shareholders cannot acquire income from a corporation which has had none to distribute and, conversely, that any assets distributed by a company which had had income must be personal income when they come into the hands of people as shareholders. Thus, given the necessary corporate earnings, directors are invested with the strange power of creating personal income in whatever amounts they may choose, and merely by a simple sort of verbal ritual. Such abuses of a venerable medium of human communication are the typical consequences of academic and judicial reflection upon that simple, homely, bookkeeper's device, the realization criterion. That such exercises in the misuse of language and rhetoric are conducive to sound judgments on questions of policy and of constitutional interpretation is rather unlikely; and, indeed, it is a miracle that to date they have yielded only occasional anomalies in income taxation instead of total confusion.

Difficulties have arisen in determining when income is received from a corporation. Famous in this connection is that

---

grams designed to restrict appropriately the powers and prerogatives of private corporations should be guided by their own proper purposes. They should be concerned with the monopoly problem, with the flagrant abuses of the corporate form, and with the abuses of the trustee position of directors and other officials. If programs of tax reform can be separated entirely from programs for reconstructing our corporation law, so much the better for both of them. It is a great fault of our existing methods of taxing personal income that they serve to mix up two basic problems of policy; and it is a great merit of the scheme here proposed that it would serve to separate them. This business of putting all kinds of special taxes on corporations can never produce good personal taxation; it does involve real diseconomies and considerable annoyance; and it serves to divert what might be a significant movement for corporation reform into endless designing of miscellaneous revenue gadgets. Taxation is the proper instrumentality for controlling the distribution of income; but it is not the proper one for controlling corporations.

engaging metaphysical treatise on the quiddity of income, *Eisner* v. *Macomber* (252 U.S. 189 ff.). Here the court deduced that stock dividends were not income, in the sense of the Sixteenth Amendment—with applause from all bookkeepers and economists. Other people also agreed with the justices; but there was a disturbing variety in the reasons adduced in support of their view. The usual argument—and one which displays some real insight—was that no gain accrued to the shareholder, that he merely acquired more pieces of paper to evidence the same fractional interest in the same equity. Some doubtful souls hastened to investigate this notion empirically and, naturally, were still in doubt after their statistical studies had been completed; but it was rarely questioned by mature people. However, even the court seemed to understand that this argument, unless wrapped up in reams of sophistry, might explode devastatingly sometime; and many people who used it must have felt uncomfortable if they were aware, or were reminded, that by this route one comes quite as readily to the astounding conclusion that cash dividends are not income either. (See Eustace Seligman, "Implications and Effects of the Stock Dividend Decision," *Columbia Law Review*, XXI, 313–33—a very stimulating article.)

The justices, and the writers whose economics they validated, relied mainly on the familiar criteria of realization and separation. To these criteria we have already paid our proper respects; but some repetition may be pardonable here. Surely few people would deny that gain is a *sine qua non* of income. Yet to conceive gain in terms of *things* received is to hypostatize an abstraction. Gain is merely a numerical result derived from intelligent manipulation of value facts. One can deduct cash paid out from cash received and ascertain the change in that asset. To conceive of income as things acquired less things parted with, however, is to contemplate the addition and subtraction of incommensurables. The decision that stock dividends should be ignored in calculating taxable income (except for the appropriate changes in the basis from which capital gains and losses are measured) was eminently sound, as a judgment about a question of legislative policy. It is most unfortunate, however, that a constitutional issue was ever raised; for brief experience with the legislation in question would almost certainly have led to general disapproval and early repeal.

As already suggested (at end of chap. iii), there is here no proper issue as to the meaning of income—only a question as to what constitutes a reasonable, consistent, and convenient application of the realization criterion; and the answer which Congress had given on this point was unfortunate and untenable. The legislation represents an early and utterly misguided effort to deal with the problem of undistributed earnings; and it would have yielded only annoyance and confusion. It would have practically prohibited the use of a valid, proper, and useful device in corporation finance. Prosperous, expanding enterprises would simply have made little or no effort to keep their shares in units convenient for stock-market trading; or perhaps they would have issued their stock dividends, as it were, by the awkward device of reorganization. Such effects would not have been calamitous, to be sure; but there would have been no offsetting gains at all.

Once the issue was raised, it was perhaps inevitable that the Court should hand down a ponderous opinion. The decision itself, while unfortunate, would have been quite innocuous; Congress would merely have lost a prerogative of acting unwisely in a matter of detail. Actually, an utterly trivial issue was made the occasion for injecting into our fundamental law a mass of rhetorical confusion which no orderly mind can contemplate respectfully, and for giving constitutional status to naïve and ridiculous notions about the nature of income and the rationale of income taxes.

Let us paraphrase briefly the language of the lawyers. Income is something separated from its capital source. "In the true sense of the term it is that which is separated from the capital while leaving the capital intact" (e.g., Professor Seligman's calf). Stock dividends are not income to the recipient because the corporation parts with no assets (the cow fails to deliver). (Here one might properly argue that tentative, provisional treatment of the dividend as income is inappropriate, even though provision were made for definitive reconciliation later on.) Cash received as a dividend is income, but only if it is distributed from earnings accumulated after 1913. If payments to shareholders are made out of capital, from depletion or depreciation reserves, or from unrealized appreciation of good-will, they are not taxable personal income (i.e., they are deductions from the basis for gain or loss calculations with respect to the stock itself; they are deductions from potential deductions, not additions to income). But distributions from a depletion reserve based on "discovery value" are taxable.

Statements like the last three above can be found in the statutes and regulations. They have a clear meaning, if one translates them accurately from the bookkeeper's code in which they are written; and they define quite unobjectionable procedures. To be sure, one might insist that receipts are just receipts and that cash dividends are paid out of cash. But this is perhaps only a matter of diction. Accountants and revenue agents have no real difficulty with these interesting devices of shorthand expression. However, when lawyers and economists try to use them (or, for that matter, when accountants themselves try to become philosophical about accounting rules), the typical results are either excruciating or disgusting, depending on whether the critical observer is seriously interested in the relevant questions of public policy. The numerical results of accounting operations are immediately reified; the discussion proceeds in terms of the income tax as a tax upon income—like a tax on potatoes or mousetraps—and loses sight of the obvious fact that it is a tax upon persons according to their respective incomes which, strictly, are merely estimates of their relative "prosperity." The attempt to label particular disbursements to shareholders as income or not-income is perfectly appropriate where one is relatively unconcerned about accurate measurement of personal income for the particular year, i.e., where one seeks only the least arbitrary and most convenient methods of *tentative, provisional* determination within a system of accounting rules which assures ultimate offsetting of errors and ultimate elimination of the element of arbitrariness. The accountant, with a little pressing, can usually promise ultimate (and often fairly prompt) correction of his crude year-to-year results (he usually practices much better than he preaches); but judges insist on taking very seriously his methods of tentative or provisional estimation and without comprehending the long-run results of his total system of rules.

The legal and statutory conception of income as things received leads to some interesting anomalies. Suppose that Mr. A purchases a share of stock of the X company for $200. On the following day the company declares (and promptly pays) a cash dividend of $100 per share, "from earnings accumulated since 1913." Mr. A thus suddenly is faced with an unexpected increase in his taxable income; he has suddenly acquired an item of income from the corporation which clearly is both realized and separated and also paid out of earnings. If time remains, Mr. A may hastily sell his stock and obtain an offsetting loss deduction. However, if he waits more than a year, his offset may be excluded by the $2,000 limitation; if he dies before selling the stock, leaving the specific property to a legatee, no offsetting deduction will ever occur; and, if he sells more than ten years later, he loses to the extent of the tax on 70 per cent of his initial "gain." All these curious limitations apart, persons of moderate means should be careful not to invest heavily in the stock of companies which might make enormous distribution from past earnings; for one enormous distribution might subject them to high surtax rates, with no possibility, under progressive annual rates, for compensating deductions afterward.

The total system of rules which our income tax comprises, however, is surprisingly superior to the general ideas which have gone into it. The craftsmen have built a fairly good structure in spite of the architects; evidently the wisdom of minor civil servants has prevented the translation of stupidity into folly. One looks hard, in the statutes or in the treasury regulations, for flaws or inconsistencies which are not wholly attributable to gross errors, of commission or of omission, in broader matters of legislative policy. If a small fraction of the effort and intelligence which has gone into small details could be focused on fundamental matters of structure or design, the results would be amazing.

The constitutional aspects of exemptions under the income tax are perhaps peculiarly ill-suited to discussion among the uninitiated; and the issues here are somewhat less critical; for the prevailing constitutional interpretation, however unwise, is of such long standing and is now so generally accepted that explicit constitutional amendment is perhaps the proper procedure for change. Even with that amendment, however, some change in the underlying rules of interpretation would be desirable. There is something weird in the reasoning whereby the Court, in the name of preserving powers reserved to the states, may require that the federal government subsidize state borrowing in order to exercise a specifically delegated power. It would be hardly less absurd to hold that all progressive personal taxes were invalid because, through their effect upon saving, they increased the costs of borrowing, to the states along with other borrowers. Taxing interest on state obligations as personal income would leave the states in exactly the same position as other borrowers; rates of interest would be unaffected, except possibly by indirection through reduction in the total supplies of loan funds available per year; and no impairment of state powers could possibly arise so long as this item of personal receipts was treated uniformly with other interest items and with other receipts generally. The proper function of the Constitution and the Court is that of providing remedies against arbitrary discrimination in the personal taxes—of protecting the states on this score, along with other parties. The rule of no taxation with respect to state instrumentalities does have a convenient definiteness and simplicity, by comparison with the proper prohibition of actually disabling, discriminatory levies; but these admirable qualities are purchased at the cost of distortion of the meaning and purpose of the Sixteenth Amendment. Incidentally, there appears to be a bit of neglected judicial insight in the decision that an income tax payable by firms engaged in exportation, along with other firms uniformly, is not a tax upon exports (*Peck* v. *Lowe*, 247 U.S. 165 ff.).

The prevailing misconceptions about income taxation, among lawyers especially, are perhaps crucially important for the future of reform schemes like the one which these chapters have sketched. Could Congress now recognize and correct the critical limitations of the realization criterion, as now applied, without creating innumerable constitutional difficulties and uncertainties? On this question the judgment of a writer unequipped with legal knowledge and unskilled in legal sophistries can have little value; but unspoiled ignorance may sometimes yield useful suggestions.

If there is any sense in our views about the nature and definition of income, then sound, critical appraisal must place the strictures of the Court in *Eisner* v. *Macomber* little above those of Professor Seligman (see chap. iii above). In both instances the whole argument is simply confusion confounded. If this decision really defines our fundamental law as to income taxes, little progress in personal taxation can be achieved without endless amendment of Court-made rules. The Court has asserted its prerogative of passing on every positive item which Congress may include in the determination of the tax base, to determine whether the item is income or not-income. This whole approach, to repeat, is merely confusing. The Sixteenth Amendment was intended to authorize not an *Ertragssteuer* but a levy upon individuals according to their respective income circumstances. This fact can only be obscured by sophistries; and it is impliedly conceded at many points by many persons who might dispute it. Thus, the only question which properly can arise, as to the constitutionality of a federal personal income tax, is whether the prescribed calculations define something which is reasonable or equitable as a basis for differential personal taxation, according to the spirit of the amendment; and the only question which may properly be raised about a particular provision of the law is whether, as part of the system of rules, it is reasonably consistent with that result.

Such interpretation, moreover, would leave the Court with

substantial powers and responsibilities. Its function would be that of affording recourse against devices of income taxation which served to discriminate clearly and arbitrarily between persons, especially between persons of the same real circumstances. There are possibilities of dangerous abuses in personal taxation; and it is appropriate that there should be clear constitutional protection against them. To provide such protection, however, the Court must recognize clearly and unambiguously that this is a *personal* tax—a tax upon persons, not a tax upon income. Moreover, the Court must look always to the workings of the rules as a whole; and it must, with the inevitable reliance on the realization criterion, look always beyond the results in any one year and consider how the rules work out through time.

The only constitutional defense which a political economist can offer for the reforms proposed in these chapters is that they are consistent with equitable relative levies upon individuals and, indeed, that they are indispensable to that end. The whole scheme is designed primarily to assure that two persons with the same total of gains and earnings during their lives will be levied upon with respect to the same total of taxable income. We have tried to show that any substantial departure from this sort of scheme is fairly certain to leave numerous opportunities for systematic avoidance. Thus, the Court should not interfere— unless it can be shown that, in some particulars, the legislation introduces substantial, systematic, and arbitrary discrimination of a kind incompatible with the spirit of the Sixteenth Amendment. From this viewpoint, incidentally, it would seem quite as proper to invalidate a legislative definition of taxable income for its omissions or exclusions as for its inclusions.

CHAPTER X

SUMMARY AND STATEMENT OF GENERAL POSITION

W E PROPOSE now to indicate concisely the main ideas and proposals of the previous nine chapters and to touch briefly on some other matters which call for comment in a proper statement of our general position on matters of taxation policy.

There is an important (though subordinate) place for strictly impersonal, *ad rem* levies in a good tax system. On the basis of the presumption against governmental subsidies to particular groups, one may argue decisively for the indefinite continuance of real-property taxes without change in the established effective rates; for continued imposition of ordinary special assessments (what are sometimes called "cost assessments"); for the heavy taxation of gasoline and other fuels used in highway transport; and for other benefit levies where reliable minimum estimates of benefits are possible and where convenient forms of levy are available. All taxes which fail of justification on these grounds may properly be judged mainly in terms (*a*) of their effects upon the degree of economic inequality and (*b*) of their fairness between and among persons of similar economic circumstances.

Such considerations point to the income tax as the proper source of those necessary revenues which cannot be provided by the few good impersonal taxes. The personal income tax should be progressive; it should be levied according to simple general rules or principles (complexity in detailed applications is, of course, unavoidable); and, subject to this latter requirement, it should be as equitable as possible among individuals. Thus, it must proceed from a clear and workable conception of personal income; and it must be constructed in such manner as to minimize the possibilities, both of lawful avoidance (defined in terms of the basic conception of income) and of successful evasion through false declarations.

The appropriate general conception of income, for purposes of personal taxation, may be defined as the algebraic sum of the individual's consumption expense and accumulation during the accounting period. Taxable income, properly, is a kind of measure of the individual's prosperity—or, in the language of Professor Haig, a measure of "the net accretion of one's economic power between two points in time" (if one includes power exercised for consumption purposes). Money affords, of course, a very imperfect unit for purposes of such measurement; but any attempt to allow systematically for monetary instability in the measurement of taxable income seems altogether inexpedient; and the establishment of a monetary system which was reasonably satisfactory in other respects would largely dispose of this special problem in personal taxation. The measurement of consumption also presents grave difficulties of principle, especially in the case of receipts in kind. These difficulties largely disappear in practice, however, when "earned income in kind" is exempted or disregarded; and the omission of such receipts is defensible not only as a concession to administrative necessity but also as a desirable offset to the disregard of leisure as a form of consumption. The measurement and inclusion of income in kind from consumer capital used by the owner presents only minor practical difficulties which can be dealt with adequately.

In principle, all receipts from gifts, inheritances, and bequests should be included in determining the basis of individual contributions under income taxes. This procedure is desirable (a) to avoid arbitrary and casuistic distinctions in the underlying definition of income, (b) to make the system more nearly foolproof by introducing a larger measure of automatic cancellation with respect to the inevitable errors in property appraisal, and (c) as part of a scheme for rescuing the whole enterprise of inheritance taxation from confusion, unfairness, and futility. Complete inclusion of all gifts, however, is unthinkable, especially in the case of small gifts in kind; tax legislation must stop short of folly, by deliberately disregarding minor gifts in most instances. Just how far and in what cases such items may wisely be disregarded is a difficult practical question; but reasonably satisfactory solutions can surely be worked out through careful experiment and experience.

The proper underlying conception of income cannot be directly and fully applied in the determination of year-to-year assessments. Outright abandonment of the realization criterion would be utter folly; no workable scheme can require that taxpayers reappraise and report all their assets annually; and, while this procedure is implied by the underlying definition of income, it is quite unnecessary to effective application of that definition. Our income taxes, as a matter of declaration, of administration, and of adjudication, rest upon great masses of business records and accounts; and they simply must follow, in the main, the established procedures of accounting practice. Thus, they must follow the realization criterion, but not so blindly and reverently as in the past. The recognition of capital gains and losses may wisely be postponed while the property remains in an owner's possession; but postponement should not be allowed to eventuate in evasion. Thus all accrued gains must be taxed as income to the individual owner whenever the property passes out of his hands, whether by sale or by gift, and as income to his estate when the property is transferred to his heirs or legatees. By such arrangements, the same total of taxable income may be reached for every taxpayer during his lifetime as would have been reached by direct application each year of the procedure implicit in our fundamental definition. The distribution of his taxable income between particular years would be different, to be sure, under the two procedures; but the taxpayer would be free so to manage his affairs that the distribution would not work greatly to his (or his heirs') disadvantage; and, apart from successful gambling on rate changes, he could not manipulate the distribution unfairly to his own advantage.[1]

[1] Rate changes apart, the best he could do would be, by timing appropriately his sales of capital assets, to equalize his annual taxable incomes, including that (those) of his estate; and no one interested in fairness would properly begrudge him that. Under present arrangements, of course, the individual's freedom to time the realizing of his gains, and of his losses es-

A strong if not decisive case can be made for not introducing the corresponding (consistent ?) provisions as to "unrealized capital losses." If deductible losses could be established by gift, there would be a strong temptation for false reporting, especially in the case of transfers to persons of smaller means or to exempt institutions; and adequate policing of the law at this point would be difficult and expensive. Moreover, the denial of deductions in such cases would only compel the taxpayer to establish his loss through bona fide sale. If this consideration is less decisive in the case of estates, the fact remains that individuals could easily protect their heirs by systematically avoiding large accumulations of potential loss deductions, i.e., by rather nominal shifting of their investments or merely by parting occasionally with particular securities for short periods (over thirty days—see sec. 118). A strictly limited deduction for unrealized losses, however, might reasonably be allowed in the case of estates—but not in the case of gifts.

Such cases apart, there should be no limitations whatever upon the deduction of bona fide losses, and no limitations or concessions with respect to the inclusion of capital gains. Any special treatment of particular gains and losses by kind is utterly incompatible with the proper purposes and functions of the income tax—just as incompatible in principle as, and more so in practice

---

pecially, does give rise both to inequity among persons and to substantial revenue losses—but only because taxable gains vanish in probate. This difficulty disappears under the arrangements which we have proposed—and with it would disappear the only plausible argument for limitation upon the deduction of capital losses or upon the inclusion of capital gains. In this connection see addendum to chap. vii above.

than, the exemption of interest on state and local debts. And any one-sided restrictions as to losses are too ridiculous and inequitable for serious consideration. That such restrictions are somewhat defensible in our present income tax only testifies to the existence of flagrant shortcomings at other points; they can find no justification as part of a good law.[2]

Other features of the general scheme of levy need be mentioned only in summary statements of specific proposals:

1. All exemptions of receipts by kind (save those of "earned income in kind" and minor gifts) should be eliminated entirely—notably, the exemption of interest on governmental obligations.

[2] One is tempted, in the immediate political situation (December, 1936), to plead fervently and prayerfully on these points; for they seem crucially important for the immediate future. The example of other countries invites further pursuit of mistaken policies here. There has long been strong pressure for more lenient treatment of capital gains; some of the leaders in Congress who could be relied upon to resist this pressure are no longer there; and the careful efforts of persons interested in widening the avenues for surtax avoidance are now supplemented by the misguided efforts of persons who see, in further limitation upon loss deductions, a means of increasing tax revenues without increasing tax rates. On the other hand, there is almost no real understanding of the issues involved, either among prominent academic students of taxation or among other persons who might marshal resistance against tragic errors of legislation.

The whole enterprise of progressive personal taxation can now be wrecked, or long and seriously disabled, by revisions of sec. 117 which many economists and almost all business men would, in the beginning at least, warmly commend. Continuance of present arrangements would be sufficiently tragic; but, given the state of the literature, of professional discussion, of public opinion, and of political leadership, it seems almost a miracle that we have not already moved farther backward—all the way instead of most of the way—toward English and Continental practices. And the prospects are now especially ominous.

The literal exemption of gains and losses from sales of capital assets, how-

2. Income in kind from the more durable forms of consumer capital used by the owner should be included in determining his taxable income, at least in the case of real property used for consumption purposes.

3. All gifts, inheritances, and bequests should be treated as part of the recipient's taxable income for the year in which they are received (with such limited and carefully devised exemptions for minor gifts as are required by administrative necessity).

---

ever defined (or the recourse to separate taxation of capital gains), would open up innumerable opportunities for the evasion of personal taxes and, indeed, would make progression almost farcical. That the arrangement has not become intolerable in England, with English lethargy and moral inhibitions about deliberate tax avoidance, and with the broad discretionary powers of the competent and scrupulous inspectors—this is no proper reason for supposing that it would not be calamitous here. When one contemplates the probable distortions of private financial arrangements, the innumerable inventions of the tax-avoidance specialists, and the endless procession of stopgap legislation to combat each new evasion trick, the picture is simply a nightmare.

There simply can be no equitable taxation of individuals according to their respective circumstances if any major kind of gains or losses is ignored in the determination of taxable personal income. Moreover, the law must prevent systematic avoidance if the income tax is ever to occupy its proper place in our fiscal system or even, perhaps, if it is to escape the fate of our personal property taxes. Its essential purpose is that of reasonable relative taxation of persons; and, if that purpose is lost in a confusion of legalistic sophistry, of amateurish manipulation of economic concepts, and of dishonest concessions to disguised demands for avoidance opportunities, then our tax will probably come to be also "eine Ertragssteuer mit Einkommensteuermomenten" or something worse. Along the lines of modifications begun in 1921, and continued in 1934, there is only more and more confusion ahead, and gradual deflection into futility of the only promising enterprise in tax reform which our most sanguine hopes can now hold out. Furthermore, if we cannot build now an abundantly productive system of equitable personal taxes, as one indispensable part of a program for preserving a democratic, free-enterprise system against the current trend back to collectivism and irresponsible political authority, then that glorious undertaking is simply hopeless.

4. A supplementary personal tax, in the cumulative form of our present tax on donors, should be levied upon the recipients of gifts, inheritances, and bequests, to eliminate any advantage which might otherwise be obtained, under a progressive annual tax, by gradual distribution of property. (Amounts actually paid as additional income tax by virtue of such receipts should be deductible from the taxes as imposed by this supplementary levy.)

5. The law should provide for full inclusion of all gains on assets which have appreciated in the owner's possession, the gains being taxable at time of bona fide sale or, at an amount determined by fair appraisal, on the occasion of any other disposition of the property. In the case of property passing through probate, any appreciation should be taxed as income to the estate in the same manner as it would have been taxed to the decedent if, living, he had given the property to the beneficiary on the date when it actually passes to the beneficiary from the estate. Full deduction should be allowed for all *realized* capital losses; but no deduction should be allowed to donors with respect to estimated losses on property transferred by gift; and only limited deductions, if any at all, should be permitted to estates with respect to assets not actually sold.

6. Rebates should be made available every five years for the amount by which an individual's income-tax payments for the last five years have exceeded, by more than 10 per cent, the total which he would have paid if his taxable income each year had been exactly

one-fifth of his total taxable income for the five-year period. (It is very doubtful whether gifts, inheritances, and bequests should be brought into the calculation, on either side, for purposes of determining such rebates.)

We submit that the scheme of personal taxation which these proposals define has many merits and no serious shortcomings which are apparent. It meets the requirement of following a few simple general rules; and it promises to be more nearly fair among persons than any other scheme which would satisfy that requirement. On the administrative side, moreover, it has merits which are likely to be underestimated. The system of rules is as nearly foolproof as possible; it provides an abundance of internal checks; and it exploits rather fully the peculiar virtues of the income-tax form, namely, the possibilities of the automatic cancelling of errors at different points in time. Taxpayers would be obliged to account for every acquisition and every disposition of property; values at time of transfer would enter into the declarations of both taxpayers; and gain and loss calculations will (almost) always proceed from a basis already reported by the previous owner. Thus, declarations will record a substantially unbroken chain of selling prices or appraisals; and falsification or error at one stage can always be compensated or at least detected at the next stage. Finally, the system would tend to alter as little as possible the course which would have been followed, if there had been no such taxes, in commercial and financial practices and in the management and distribution of private wealth; and it would minimize the diseconomies arising from the continuous and disturbing enactment of stopgap expedients for dealing with the inventions of tax-avoidance specialists.[3]

It should be immediately obvious that no such scheme of personal taxation could effectively be employed by the individual American states. The states lack adequate jurisdiction; and effective enforcement not only is unattainable by the states but, if attained, would involve an extravagant duplication of administrative machinery and administrative activities—not to mention the dangers of cutthroat competition to hold and attract persons of wealth. The broad jurisdictional powers of the federal government are indispensable, as is an integrated national organization for administration and enforcement. The states are reasonably competent to im-

[3] The simplicity and elegance of the underlying principles would also be conducive to solution of many vexed problems which we have not referred to previously. Take, for example, the problem of legal trusts. If transfers were taxable under the income tax both as gifts to (nonrevocable) trusts and as gifts from trusts to the beneficiaries, then this legal device would not be very attractive as a means for avoidance; nor would legitimate uses of the trust device be penalized, since the levies would properly not be imposed in the case of revocable trusts or in cases where the arrangements permitted full taxation of the beneficiaries with respect to the income of the trust and, whether ultimately or immediately, with respect to the capital gift as income. In other words, double taxation of the gifts would occur only in the case of trusts created for tax-free accumulation (i.e., to obtain lower rates of tax by the separation). Again, take the case of the community-property problem. Here, a husband and wife might be permitted the saving of income tax which the special laws of their state may permit, but only provided income tax had been paid with respect to gifts just as though an explicit and deliberate division of property had been effected. This need involve no inversion of the present discrimination in favor of the residents of community-property states, for persons undertaking to report for income tax without benefit of the state laws might be exempted from tax with respect to the division of property until that division was effected through probate or through definitive marriage settlement. Many complicated difficulties with respect to life insurance contracts might also be eliminated.

pose real-property taxes, special assessments, highway taxes, and license charges; but it should be evident, even without the eloquent testimony of experience, that they cannot contribute much to the development of equitable personal taxes.

On the other hand, the kind of levies which represent the proper contributions of the state and local bodies to our total system of taxes are inadequate to their expenditure responsibilities. Many of them could not abandon their existing income taxes and death duties without serious disarrangement of their finances; and most states now rely largely upon undesirable revenue devices. The only promising solution thus lies in a generous sharing of federal revenues from personal taxes with the states.

But would this not involve a thoroughly dangerous measure of federal centralization—a dangerous increase in federal powers at the expense of the states? The question may properly give us pause. The maintenance of a vital sort of state and local government, and the reservation of large freedom and large responsibilities to the smaller jurisdictions, are indispensable for the preservation of representative political institutions. Special students of the various kinds of governmental activities are prone to urge, each in the field of his own special study, a measure of centralization which, if achieved in all the special fields, would reduce state and local government almost to sheer ceremony. Everyone seems to want a degree of centralization, in those activities which are objects of his special interest, far larger than a wise economy of centralizing devices could possibly grant. Do we not offend here on this score, losing sight of larger interests in our zeal for equitable personal taxation and mitigation of inequality?

Any judgment on this point by one who confesses to such special interests may properly be received with a presumption of bias—although the study of fiscal policy is perhaps more conducive to balanced views on such matters than are other specialties. There are grave dangers here; but we submit that the scheme *could* be carried out in such manner as to yield only good results. First of all, the federal government must eschew arrangements which would enable it, through the distributions, to influence state and local policies (except perhaps in matters of income and inheritance taxation). Conditional grants-in-aid are unobjectionable so long as they involve only modest contributions to worthy causes. Such devices are totally undesirable, however, in connection with distributions of the magnitude here in question. The revenues from the personal taxes should be shared unconditionally; and the rules determining the relative shares should be designed to prevent both discretionary, administrative manipulation and frequent or substantial alteration by future Congresses. In other words, the initial legislation should serve to settle definitely the basic question of policy.

From this viewpoint, only one basis of distribution seems to merit consideration: every state should receive the same fraction of the revenues collected from taxpayers subject to its jurisdiction.[4] The tax being a purely

---

[4] A strong case can be made for sharing only the proceeds of the normal tax or, in other words, for allocating the total distributions among the states on the basis of collections under the normal tax rather than on the basis of total collections of normal tax and surtaxes. This arrangement might

personal levy, the jurisdictional basis is residence or domicile; and, while the basic principle raises hard questions in some cases, it appears to afford an adequate general rule. Marginal cases may require complicated procedures and awkward compromises of conflicting claims; but they are unlikely to defy tolerable solution or to bulk large enough in total to threaten the stability of the underlying policy. This policy would appear to be the only alternative to chaos; to have Congress struggling indefinitely over the division of, say, three billion dollars annually among the various state treasuries would be dreadful and intolerable. This is a danger of the scheme; but the very magnitude of the danger would probably assure scrupulous and co-operative efforts to avoid it.

The objective should be that of effecting the same relative distribution of revenues as would obtain (except for jurisdictional and administrative difficulties) if every state imposed the tax with the same base, the same personal exemptions, and the same scale of rates. We might thus achieve arrangements which, besides enforcing a necessary uniformity among the states, would involve substantial centralization only as regards the technical administration and enforcement of the tax.

---

seem more reasonable to most people and, thus, might prove more stable and enduring politically. It would serve to diminish the fluctuations, as between years of prosperity and depression, in the amounts received by the states and, fortunately, to increase the fluctuations of the residual federal revenues. Moreover, it would make the relative payments to the different states less dependent on the cases of a few large taxpayers. Conflicting claims might thus be less numerous, and less difficult of adjudication or compromise, than they would be if the allocations were based on total income-tax collections.

And this kind of centralization seems nowise ominous as regards the independence and responsibility of our state and local bodies. They would be left in full control of their spending activities and under the necessity of providing most of their revenues from their own tax levies.[5]

Let us now turn briefly to questions of the rates of tax. Chapter i attempts to state a straightforward case for progression and to argue that the optimum degree of progression would involve heavy rates of tax in the upper brackets It is not inconsistent, however, to suggest that progression has gone to seed rather ludicrously in our federal taxes. We have been so preoccupied with dramatic levies upon fabulous incomes and estates that we have almost forgotten to tax the large ones at all. When one considers the proportion of governmental expenditures to the national income, our income (and estate) taxes, except for a mere handful of taxpayers at the top, are simply trivial. Congressional committees and treasury experts, when proposing revenue measures, should remind themselves of what our income distribu-

---

[5] The foregoing argument relates, of course, to a very special problem. Accepting it, one may still approve moderate distributions of federal funds, for special purposes, on a per capita basis or on the basis of special formulas. Certainly, distributions on the basis of relative needs may properly have a larger place in the fiscal systems of our states. The dangers of centralization which such distributions involve obviously become less acute as one proceeds from a great federal system to smaller political jurisdictions and subdivisions. But in our vast nation these dangers, with respect to federal action, are likely to be underestimated and, in many quarters, are now almost ignored. Incidentally, the experience of England and Germany with grants-in-aid and similar devices, whether it appears to recommend the practices in question or not, is certainly more useful as a guide for policy within our individual states than as a guide for federal or national policy in this country.

tion actually is, instead of reflecting on their own conceptions of a modest living. Exemptions appear to be determined on the assumption that rates will be 100 per cent, and rates, in turn, as though there would be no exemptions. The result is a decorative sort of progression, yielding much discussion, much indignation, and very little revenue—and a total revenue system resting largely on taxes borne by persons far below the level of the income-tax exemptions. Moreover, the whole procedure involves a subtle kind of moral and political dishonesty. One senses here a grand scheme of deception, whereby enormous surtaxes are voted in exchange for promises that they will not be made effective. Thus, politicians may point with pride to the rates, while quietly reminding their wealthy constituents of the loopholes. If we had a more moderate sort of progression —a scale of rates which responsible leaders really approved—it would be less difficult to obtain the urgently necessary changes in the basis of levy. It is high time for Congress to quit this ludicrous business of dipping deeply into great incomes with a sieve.

For the future, the main question is whether our taxes shall fall mainly on people with incomes ranging from $3,000 to $20,000 or largely on people below the $2,000 level. What happens to the rates beyond $20,000 is not of major importance. This is not to say that rates are now excessive in the upper brackets (although they may be higher than the opinion of their time will support effectively); only that they are absurdly low in the case of what conventional discussion strangely refers to as the lower and middle-sized incomes.

One hears much talk about the desirability of lowering the personal exemptions. This change would increase the administrative burden enormously; and little moral gain can derive from trivial levies upon millions of persons. We need to realize that exemptions greatly reduce the effective rates for most persons now subject to the tax and to see that large exemptions and low initial rates simply do not belong in the same law. The normal tax alone should provide the great bulk of our income-tax revenues.

To complete the summary of specific proposals, we may now add three to the six already listed:

7. The rates of tax in the lower brackets should be sharply increased, with an initial rate of about 20 per cent, but without increase of the effective rates at the top of the scale. (The existing exemption for single persons and the existing credits for dependents should be retained, but the joint exemption for married persons should be reduced to $2,000.)

8. Federal revenues from the normal tax (the initial or basic rate) should be shared equally with the states, on the basis of collections, i.e., on the basis of taxpayer residence or domicile.

9. Save for the gasoline taxes and certain levies desirable for regulatory purposes, all excises, tariff duties, license taxes, and other miscellaneous regressive levies should be eliminated from both federal and state tax systems.

These nine proposals define our proximate conception of the taxation millennium.

ADDENDUM

Let us now anticipate a special objection to our proposals which may be supported by the authority of every reputable textbook in the field. Is not our scheme grossly unmindful of the canon that a good tax system must be highly stable, regular, and reliable as to yield? Certainly the full inclusion of capital gains would produce great bulges of revenue during periods of unusual business prosperity; and the full deduction of losses would greatly aggravate the decline of collections during depressions—not to mention the decline of death-rates and of gift transfers in such periods, and the effect of the averaging rebates. Have we not contrived a system which would maximize, rather than minimize, the amplitude of revenue fluctuations?

One might answer that these are simply unfortunate effects which must be accepted as the necessary cost of equitable and effective control over the distribution of economic power. Such a reply, however, would concede the wisdom of a contention which is as spurious and superficial as it is trite and commonplace. Most of the sober generalizations about "the characteristics of a good tax system" are simply innocuous verbalisms, serving mainly to disillusion the competent student about the wisdom of economists; but the proposition in question enjoys the distinction of being meaningful and, to that extent, of being wrong. It is not a fault of our scheme that it would lead to wide fluctuations of annual revenues; indeed, it is one of its greatest merits.

Proper argument in support of this position would carry us immediately into the fundamental questions of monetary policy and monetary reform; and this is not the place for systematic discussion of such questions. Here we can only indicate in a general way what the underlying argument is.[6]

The whole problem of public borrowing and of budgetary policy is fundamentally a monetary problem. To anyone familiar

[6] For argument which may adequately support the position see the writer's article, "Rules versus Authorities in Monetary Policy," *Journal of Political Economy*, XLIV, No. 1 (February, 1936), 1–30.

with recent experience or with the relevant (and substantial) economic literature, it should be indisputably clear that the implementation of monetary policy is and must be primarily fiscal. Once a deflation has gotten under way, in a large modern economy, there is no significant limit which the decline of prices and employment cannot exceed, if the central government fails to use its fiscal powers generously and deliberately to stop that decline. Only great government deficits can check the hoarding of lawful money and the destruction of money substitutes, once a general movement has gotten under way. While the technical limits of cumulative movements are more nearly significant in the case of upswings or booms, the proper checks in this direction also are to be found in the taxing, borrowing, and spending activities of the national government. Thus, fiscal policy cannot be separated from monetary (or banking) policy, however convenient the separation might be for academic specialists. We must talk about budgetary problems as monetary problems (and vice versa) or talk irrelevant nonsense about them both.

Sound monetary reform must seek primarily to minimize the economic uncertainties which have to do with general monetary conditions and disturbances. It must therefore be based on simple, reasonable, general rules which can be firmly intrenched in popular sentiments and strongly supported not only by the feeling that they are fair but also by an awareness of the need for stability and certainty. The proper means for implementing such rules, moreover, is to be found in the powers of the government to inject and withdraw money (and effective money substitutes) through exercise of its spending, taxing, and borrowing prerogatives.

The propriety of extraordinary spending in periods of low revenues and acute depression is now generally conceded—except in quarters where political antipathies are fanatical; and we give lip service to the notion that governments should curtail expenditures during booms. The technical and political difficulties of following sound practice, in these matters, can never be solved until we are committed to precise, legislative rules as guides for immediate action. But our flagrant inconsistencies in practice are out of keeping even with that large measure of underlying confusion which still prevails. We blithely raise taxes when we are trying to reflate; and we shall probably continue to regard a revenue surplus as the signal for tax reductions.

A serious criticism which can be made of recent federal budgetary policies is that the large deficit was obtained exclusively through expenditures and in spite of tax legislation. What is needed during depressions is deficits, not expenditures; and deficits may properly be obtained by tax reductions as well as through emergency outlays. With a good tax system, large deficits would appear opportunely and automatically; and the government might be spared the role of the drunken (yet politically wise) sailor with a bulging purse. Adequate reflationary deficits could be obtained without tossing money recklessly in all directions, without reliance on the hurried schemes of frenzied bureaucrats, without the numerous disadvantages of "emergency public works," and without the awful prospect of fiscal reflation carried far beyond the time when it should be reversed.

A properly sensitive revenue system would probably afford opportune and adequate reflation with only the moderate and necessary emergency appropriations for direct relief; and it would provide abundant opportunities for the timely withdrawal and sterilization of effective moneys. These opportunities, of course, might be squandered in larger expenditures (and debt retirements) that would feed the flames. This danger, however, is likely to be diminished rather than increased by tax reforms which obviously would demand a longer view in budgetary plans. During booms we shall henceforth find greater pressure for caution in governmental spending, merely by virtue of the awareness that depressions require great increases in the public debt; and that pressure would certainly be increased if the revenue system were deliberately made more responsive to changes in business conditions. There must be a sort of trustee conception of political responsibilities with respect to the revenues of prosperous years; and, while this can be assured only by mandatory, monetary rules, appropriate changes in the tax system would serve to focus attention on the dangers of shortsightedness in the management of the federal debt.[7]

Thus, the kind of personal tax which we have called ideal in other respects is also ideal from a monetary viewpoint. It is indeed the proper fiscal complement of good rules of monetary policy. Moreover, where there are no such rules (no monetary system at all), adoption of the proposed revenue arrangements would serve to improve budgetary policies and to carry us forward toward satisfactory and definitive solution of our grave monetary difficulties.

[7] If the federal government does share its tax collections generously with the states, a strong case can be made on monetary (as well as upon other) grounds for setting both maximum and minimum limits upon the total amounts which the states may receive. The states would then be assured of fairly stable revenues; and the economy would be somewhat protected against their large spending during booms, against their inopportune retrenchments and, especially, against the aggravations of their emergency excises. This arrangement, moreover, would serve to concentrate the control and management of government debts in the hands of the federal government which, as the repository of monetary powers and responsibilities, should dominate at least those operations in borrowing and debt retirement which are associated with the cyclical fluctuations of governmental revenues. Imposing upper and lower limits upon the totals distributed, of course, would require no alteration of the rules determining the relative shares of the different states.

SUPPLEMENTARY NOTE

SOME COMMENTS ON PROFESSOR FISHER'S PROPOSALS

W̲E HAVE already discussed (chap. iii) Professor Irving Fisher's views regarding the definition of income. His definition, making income synonymous with consumption, is clear and unambiguous. While it involves radical departure from traditional usage, no one should question Fisher's prerogative of defining terms as he sees fit, for the purposes of formulating and expounding a general theory of interest. Whether his special usage is justified is a question to be answered in terms of the soundness and significance of the general theory and the elegance of its exposition. While this is not the place to consider that question, it may be suggested that Professor Fisher would be dissatisfied with an *ad hoc* justification along these lines. He evidently believes that other usages of the word "income" lead inevitably to confusion and error not only in the field of capital theory but everywhere else; and he would like to extirpate these other usages completely. His latest efforts in this direction concern the income tax.

A recent essay, "Income in Theory and Income Taxation in Practice,"[1] restates his views on the meaning of income and outlines proposals for income-tax reform. This essay, like Fisher's other writing, defines

[1] *Econometrica*, V, No. 1 (January, 1937), 1-55.

his position clearly and straightforwardly. What he proposes is simply the substitution of a spendings tax, of the kind once advocated by the late Ogden Mills,[2] for the existing tax on personal income. This, of course, is a radical proposal—more radical now than when it was made by Mills—which will suggest why we have not discussed it in the preceding pages. With Fisher's special terminology, to be sure, a spendings tax may be called an income tax; but argument about the proper referent of a word should not obscure the fact that Fisher is urging us to abandon the best part of an established revenue system and to start anew with an untried form of personal tax.

If his scheme were to obtain an important political following, the opposition might well begin by renaming the existing tax and calling it, in accordance with the language of Fisher's interest theory, an earnings tax. This concession might serve to focus attention upon significant issues. To an unsympathetic critic, Fisher's main point still seems to be that anything which is called an income tax ought to be a tax on what Fisher calls income. His radical proposal, though clearly stated, is not supported by appropriate argument. He has not compared the two types of levy in terms of major considerations of fiscal policy.[3] He has not sought to define

[2] See his article, "The Spending Tax," *Bulletin of the National Tax Association*, October, 1921, pp. 18–20.

[3] In criticizing existing procedures as to capital gains and losses, he says (*op. cit.*, p. 48): "the loss taking reduces taxes at the very time that the government most needs revenue." Fisher's resort to this common argument is doubtless a matter of sheer inadvertence, for it is inconsistent with everything he has written about monetary policy.

clearly the type of levy which he is arguing against;[4] and the description of his own scheme is inadequate for purposes of critical appraisal. In principle, the scheme is clear enough; but its practical implications, especially as regards procedures of administration and enforcement, are extremely obscure. This, of course, is not entirely Fisher's fault; for there is no experience to illuminate the practical problems.

A spendings tax is presumably a tax upon persons according to their annual consumption or consumption expense. In practice, however, the base of the tax would probably have to be determined as income *minus* savings, with negative savings or capital consumption counting as a positive item. Fisher seems to contemplate a more straightforward procedure of calculation which would depart widely from established business practices of income accounting; but, given such departure, the tax would probably be unenforceable. One great merit of traditional income taxation lies in the possibility of checking declarations against business records in the form of gain-and-loss accounting; and a workable spendings tax would have to be set up in such manner as to facilitate the same kind of checking. So,

[4] In a popular article ("A Practical Schedule for an Income Tax," *The Tax Magazine*, July 1937, pp. 1–13) Fisher does refer to the Haig definition of income (p. 13 n.); but the criticisms with which he seeks to dismiss it are rather lame. One criticism vaguely invokes the illusory difficulty of double-counting; the other merely raises the difficult question about depreciation or depletion charges in the case of personal-service incomes. Certainly it is arithmetical nonsense to say, in the latter connection: "Literally applied, therefore, Professor Haig's definition would make out most people's income to be negative." What is the system of charging depreciation whereby the annual charges, in most cases, will exceed the annual use value or rental value of the depreciating asset?

a feasible type of spendings tax would appear to involve all the present problems of estimating annual income and those of measuring net annual saving or dissaving as well. In principle, the additional complication is small. Actually, however, it appears to preclude reliance on the realization criterion and, thus, to involve all the difficulties of an income-tax procedure which necessitated annual revaluation of all investment assets.

Professor Pigou, who is exceedingly sympathetic toward the exemption of savings, has sensed the practical difficulties. He says:

If savings were exempted, dishonest citizens might save in one year, thus escaping taxation, and secretly sell out and spend their savings in the next year. The skill of revenue officials in this country has succeeded in mastering many forms of dishonesty, but the opinion is widely held among experienced administrators that this form would prove too much for them; that so wide a door for evasion would be opened as seriously to impair the efficiency of the income tax as an engine of revenue.[5]

There are other difficulties which can only be suggested here. The Fisher scheme, greatly narrowing the tax base, would aggravate the problem with respect to income in kind, especially as regards services from consumer capital used by its owners. Fisher gives considerable attention to the relevant calculations. One feels, however, that his discussion never quite comes to grips with the administrative problem; and, as we have already suggested (chap. v), the best solutions are likely to be poor enough. A similar aggravation of existing difficulties would appear to be involved with respect to

5 A. C. Pigou, *A Study in Public Finance* (London, 1928), p. 140.

allowances for dependents and differentiation according to family circumstances.

There is also the question of how a spendings tax could be co-ordinated with the taxation of inheritance. With respect to the income tax, the requisite co-ordination does seem to be attainable, along the lines suggested in chapter vi; but no corresponding opportunities are apparent in the other case. There would surely be grounds for complaint if we taxed inheritances heavily and then levied again on the beneficiaries when they consumed the inherited capital. Indeed, we could expect a lot of squawking from persons who chose, or were obliged, to live beyond their incomes, and rather tolerant attitudes toward their efforts at evasion.

One may raise question on broader grounds as to the wisdom of graduating personal taxes according to consumption rather than according to a more inclusive measure of economic power. It is plausible to say that those who reinvest large incomes are merely custodians of wealth for the community; and no reasonable person will question the moral superiority of such behavior as against vulgar and tasteless ostentation in private consumption. But there is an urgent social and political problem of preventing excessive and persisting inequality of power. Our private sentiments may properly distinguish between better and worse uses of great economic power; but these distinctions should not blind us to the need for mitigating inequality or to the danger that our efforts in this direction will miscarry if we attempt to differentiate greatly among persons according to the way in which they use their power.

This brings us to the important question of tax rates. To obtain under the spendings tax the same degree of progression that we now have, or the same amount of taxes on persons of great wealth, would require maximum surtax rates of several hundred per cent—or, apart from unnecessary avoidance opportunities, perhaps of 1,000 per cent. It is reasonably certain, of course, that such equivalent rates would not be imposed under the spendings tax—which will commend the scheme in some quarters. Moreover, if such rates were imposed, the difficulties which we have mentioned above would surely assume serious proportions.

While we may exaggerate the inherent administrative difficulties of a spendings tax, it is hard to avoid understatement in arguing against revolutionary change in existing arrangements. Long experience, here and abroad, has taught us much about problems of income taxation and about the opportunities for salutary reforms. We have achieved and preserved a high level of taxpayer morality and taxpayer co-operation; we have gradually developed a system of administrative procedures and techniques of enforcement which, after drastic change in the form of levy, we probably could not rebuild to a similar level of effectiveness within a generation. Given a revenue system which, at many other points, does need drastic changes, it would be folly to start over from the beginning with our income tax or to discard the essential structure of established methods and procedures.

Professor Fisher is pleading sincerely for a different form of personal tax; but there is no movement whatever for the adoption of his scheme. Thus his efforts now serve only to strengthen another movement whose success would ruin or impair the existing basis for progressive taxation without substituting any other sensible basis. The pressure groups which his writings actually support want neither a good income tax (earnings tax) along traditional lines nor a good spendings tax. What they want is simply larger loopholes for avoidance and wider discrepancies between the nominal rates and the effective rates in our progressive taxes.

INDEX

Ability to pay, 5, 17, 31, 41 n., 62, 139

Accountants, meaning of income to, 80 ff., 200 f.

Accrual: notation of, as to income, 83, 99 f.; procedures, 105 n.

Accumulation, 24, 26, 29, 95, 97, 145 f.; and personal income, 49 ff., 89 ff.

Adams, H. C., 16 n.

Ad rem taxation, 5, 31 ff., 128, 131, 151, 161, 163, 167, 168, 187, 188, 205

Allix et Lecercle, 75 n.

Ammon, A., 48 n., 58 n.

Australian income tax, 117

Averaging devices, 153 f., 212 f.

Avoidance: capital gains, special treatment of, and, 172; and community property, 214 n.; and corporate form, 185; systematic versus fortuitous, 107 f.; and tax-exempt securities, 172; trusts, use of for, 214 n. *See also* Evasion

Bauckner, A., 56 n., 60 n., 75

Benefit, taxation according to, 3 ff.

Benefit levies, 34 ff., 205

Bequests. *See* Gifts, Gratuitous receipts, *and* Inheritance taxation

Budgetary policy, income taxation and, 221–24

Cannan, Edwin, 94 n.

Canning, J. B., 91 n., 98 n., 120

Capital accumulation: effect of government debt reduction on, 27 n.; effect of progression on, 21 ff.; and government ownership of utilities, 27 n.; government as saver and, 27 ff. *See also* Accumulation

Capital gains, 148–69, 207–12; in American legislation, 158 ff.; ap-portionment of undivided profits and calculation of, 193 f.; and avoidance opportunities, 152 f., 185; constitutional problems as to, 203 ff.; English law as to, 148, 150, 210 n.; French law as to, 148; German law as to, 149 f.; gift, inheritance, or bequest, property acquired by, and, 147 n., 162 ff., 207 ff.; irregularity of income and, 151 ff.; and maximum-revenue criterion, 156; partnerships, corporations treated as, and, 185; and price-level changes, 155 ff.; real versus nominal, 155; special treatment of, case against, 155 ff., 210 n.; and undivided corporate profits, 157, 185

Capital losses, limitation upon deduction of, 20 n., 159 f., 162, 209. *See also* Capital gains

Cassel, Gustav, 45 n.

Centralization, fiscal, 214 ff.

Clark, J. B., 12

Cohen-Stuart, A. J., 6

Cohn, Gustav, 65

Colm, G., 104 n., 105 n.

Colwyn Committee, 137 n., 141

Committee, Joint, on Internal Revenue Taxation, 147 n., 157 n., 160 ff.

Committee on National Debt and Taxation. *See* Colwyn Committee

Commodity taxes, 34, 38, 39

Community property, 214 n.

Compensation, in kind, 122 ff; versus gifts, as income, 134 f.

Competitive free trade, vii

Constitutional questions, 171, 173 n., 196–204

Consumer capital, income to owner from, 112 ff.; Australian practice

233